KE

CONSUMER LAW

JACQUELINE MARTIN
CHRIS TURNER

HODDER
EDUCATION
PART OF HACHETTE LIVRE UK

Orders: please contact Bookpoint Ltd, 130 Milton Park, Abingdon, Oxon OX14 4SB.
Telephone: (44) 01235 827720. Fax: (44) 01235 400454. Lines are open from 9.00–5.00,
Monday to Saturday, with a 24-hour message answering service.
You can also order through our website: www.hoddereducation.co.uk

British Library Cataloguing in Publication Data
A catalogue record for this title is available from The British Library.

ISBN 978 0 340 88758 5

First published 2005
Impression number   10 9 8 7 6 5 4
Year   2010 2009 2008

Hachette Livre UK's policy is to use papers that are natural, renewable and recyclable products
and made from wood grown in sustainable forests. The logging and manufacturing processes
are expected to conform to the environmental regulations of the country of origin.

Typeset by Transet Limited, Coventry, England.
Printed in Great Britain for Hodder Education, part of Hachette Livre UK, 338 Euston Road,
London NW1 3BH by CPI Cox & Wyman, Reading, RG1 8EX.

CONTENTS

PREFACE

The Key Facts series is designed to give a clear view of each subject. This will be useful to students when tackling new topics and is invaluable as a revision aid. Most chapters open with an outline in diagram form of the points covered in that chapter. The points are then developed in list form to make learning easier. Supporting cases are given throughout by name, and for some complex areas the facts of cases are given to reinforce the point being made.

The topics covered for Consumer Law include the protections given to consumers through the law of contract and tort, statutory protection given in such areas as unsolicited goods, distance selling, defective goods, trade description, misleading prices and consumer credit. Consumer Law is a practical and useful subject in the modern world.

The law is as we believe it to be at 1st January 2005.

CHAPTER 1

INTRODUCTION TO CONSUMER PROTECTION

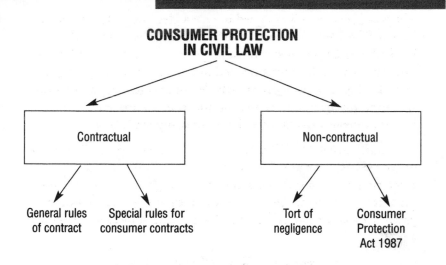

CONSUMER PROTECTION IN CIVIL LAW

Contractual

Non-contractual

General rules of contract

Special rules for consumer contracts

Tort of negligence

Consumer Protection Act 1987

1.1 INTRODUCTION

1. Consumers are protected by both civil and criminal law.
2. The general law of contract gives some protection, especially from misrepresentation (see Chapter 2).
3. There are special rules for consumer contracts. These include:
   - contracts for buying goods (see Chapter 3);
   - contracts for services (see Chapter 6);
   - distance selling (see Chapter 5);
   - other specialist area such as package holidays, insurance, food and finance.
4. The tort of negligence gives limited protection where the consumer has no contractual rights (see Chapter 7).
5. There is protection from defective goods under the Consumer Protection Act 1987 (see Chapter 11).
6. The criminal law gives protection against such matters as false

trade descriptions (see Chapter 12) and misleading prices (see Chapter 13).
7. Consumer finance is protected (see Chapter 14).
8. The Office of Fair Trading has powers in respect of adverse consumer practices.

1.2 THE NEED FOR CONSUMER PROTECTION

1. Contract law is generally based on the freedom of the individual to make whatever contract he wishes.
2. In consumer law it used to be thought that no one supplier or producer could dominate the market and so competition would keep prices and quality reasonable.
3. However, in consumer contracts it is recognised that, in today's world of multi-national companies, there is an imbalance of power between such companies and the consumer.
4. Businesses often use standard term forms for their contracts and an individual does not really have the choice of altering those terms.
5. For this reason, the law implies terms in consumer contracts and ensures that those terms cannot be excluded by businesses as against consumers.
6. It is necessary to protect the general public from harmful or dangerous items.
7. It is also necessary to give protection from malpractice such as misleading prices.

1.3 CONSUMER CONTRACTS

1. In order for there to be a consumer contract, there must be:
   - one party dealing as a consumer; and
   - another party acting in the course of business.
2. In addition, in some contracts, the goods must be of a type ordinarily supplied for private use or consumption.

1.3.1 Dealing as a consumer

1. There is no statutory definition of 'consumer'; although various acts use the phrase 'dealing as a consumer'.
2. The most useful dictionary definition of a 'consumer' is 'someone who buys goods and services for personal use or need' (*Chambers' 21st Century Dictionary*).
3. It has been argued that 'consumer' should be equated with 'citizen' and that consumer protection law should be regarded as an aspect of civic rights (Ralph Nader, US).
4. The Unfair Contract Terms Act 1977 (UCTA) s12(1)(a) states that 'a person deals as a consumer if the other party is unable to prove that he neither makes the contract in the course of business nor holds himself out as doing so'.
5. A company can be a 'consumer' where the purchase is not for some definite business purpose and is one which is not made regularly by that company (*R & B Customs Brokers Co Ltd v United Dominions Trust Ltd* (1988)).
6. The Unfair Terms in Consumer Contracts Regulations 1999 (SI 1999/2083) apply only in favour of a 'natural person … acting for purposes outside his trade or profession' (reg 3(1)).
7. UCTA s12(2), as amended by the Sale and Supply of Goods to Consumers Regulations 2002, means that a person who purchases at an auction sale is not regarded as a consumer where:
   - he is an individual and the goods are second-hand goods sold at a public auction at which individuals have the opportunity of attending the sale in person; or
   - he is not an individual.

1.3.2 Supplier acting in the course of business

1. The phrase 'in the course of business' is used in both criminal and civil law.
2. The courts have tried to keep the meaning consistent across both criminal and civil law, as where *R & B Customs Brokers*

Co Ltd v United Dominion Trust Ltd (1988) (a civil case) followed the guidance in *Davies v Sumner* (1984) (a criminal case).

3. The transaction must be an integral part of the business: eg selling a car was held to be an integral part of a car-hire business as it was part of its normal practice to buy and dispose of cars (*Havering LBC v Stevenson* (1970)).

4. A sale can be 'in the course of business' even though the seller does not habitually trade in goods of the type in question (*Ashington Piggeries Ltd v Christopher Hill Ltd* (1972)).

5. There must be some degree of regularity (*Davies v Sumner* (1984)).

6. In *Stevenson v Rogers* (1999) it was accepted that there are three broad categories used to identify when a sale is in the course of business. These are:
   - the sale is in the nature of trade carried out with a view to a profit, even if it is a one-off venture;
   - where the transaction is integral to the business carried on by the seller;
   - where the transaction is incidental to the business carried on by the seller but the type of transaction concerned is undertaken with a degree of regularity.

7. Work performed as a hobby, with no significant profit, is not in the course of business (*Blakemore v Bellamy* (1983)).

1.3.3 Private use or consumption

1. Some statutory provisions add a further requirement in order for a transaction to be recognised as a consumer one. This is that the goods or services must be intended for non-business or for consumer use.

2. The goods do not have to be used exclusively by consumers to be capable of being intended for non-business or for consumer use.

3. For s12(1)(c) UCTA this rule no longer applies where the person claiming to 'deal as a consumer' is an individual (reg 14 Sale and Supply of Goods to Consumers Regulations 2002).

CONSUMER	BUSINESS
Dealing as a consumer • contract not made in course of business • not holding himself out as acting in course of business • a company can be a consumer • but 1999 regulations only apply to natural person acting outside his trade or profession	**In the course of business** • transaction an integral part of business • some degree of regularity • in the nature of trade and carried out with a view to a profit
Exception Individual buying second-hand goods at auction is not a consumer where public can attend	**Exception** Carried out as a hobby, with no significant profit

1.4 NON-CONTRACTUAL CONSUMERS

1. Where the ultimate consumer was not a party to the contract, there is no protection under the law of contract.
2. Such consumers may be able to rely on the limited rights in the law of negligence (*Donoghue v Stevenson* (1932)).
3. Where the goods are defective, there is consumer protection in a non-contractual situation under the Consumer Protection Act 1987, where the consumer has suffered personal injury or damages of more than £75.

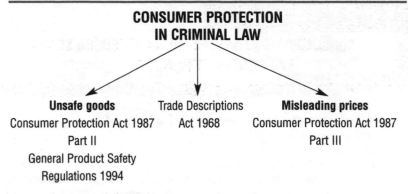

CONSUMER PROTECTION IN CRIMINAL LAW

Unsafe goods
Consumer Protection Act 1987
Part II
General Product Safety
Regulations 1994

Trade Descriptions
Act 1968

Misleading prices
Consumer Protection Act 1987
Part III

1.5 PROTECTION UNDER THE CRIMINAL LAW

1. The Consumer Protection Act 1987 and the General Product Safety Regulations 1994 create criminal offences in respect of unsafe goods.
2. The Trade Descriptions Act 1968 makes it a criminal offence to apply a false trade description in the course of trade or business.
3. It also makes it an offence to supply or offer to supply goods to which a false trade description has been applied.
4. Part III of the Consumer Protection Act 1987 creates offences in relation to misleading prices.

1.6 ADMINISTRATIVE CONTROL

1. The Fair Trading Act 1973 and the Enterprise Act 2002 set down rules on adverse consumer practices.
2. The Office of Fair Trading and local trading standards departments can issue orders against traders and apply for the enforcement of orders when breaches continue.

CHAPTER 2

CONSUMER PROTECTION IN CONTRACT LAW

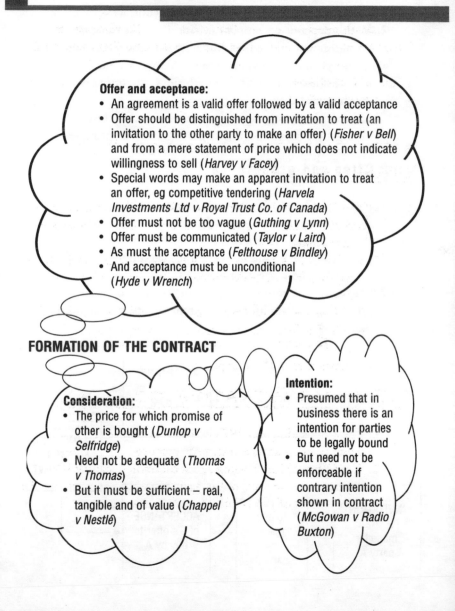

Offer and acceptance:
- An agreement is a valid offer followed by a valid acceptance
- Offer should be distinguished from invitation to treat (an invitation to the other party to make an offer) (*Fisher v Bell*) and from a mere statement of price which does not indicate willingness to sell (*Harvey v Facey*)
- Special words may make an apparent invitation to treat an offer, eg competitive tendering (*Harvela Investments Ltd v Royal Trust Co. of Canada*)
- Offer must not be too vague (*Guthing v Lynn*)
- Offer must be communicated (*Taylor v Laird*)
- As must the acceptance (*Felthouse v Bindley*)
- And acceptance must be unconditional (*Hyde v Wrench*)

FORMATION OF THE CONTRACT

Consideration:
- The price for which promise of other is bought (*Dunlop v Selfridge*)
- Need not be adequate (*Thomas v Thomas*)
- But it must be sufficient – real, tangible and of value (*Chappel v Nestlé*)

Intention:
- Presumed that in business there is an intention for parties to be legally bound
- But need not be enforceable if contrary intention shown in contract (*McGowan v Radio Buxton*)

2.1 FORMATION OF CONTRACTS

2.1.1 Introduction to formation

1. A consumer must first establish that a contract actually exists.

2. So this depends on proper formation – there must be:
- agreement – based on mutuality over the terms, agreement exists when a valid **acceptance** follows a valid offer;
- consideration – given by both sides, the *quid pro quo*, and the proof that the bargain exists;
- intention to create legal relations – since a contract is legally enforceable, unlike mere gratuitous promises.

2.1.2 Offer and acceptance

1. A contract usually begins with acceptance of an offer. An offer is a statement by one party (the **offeror** – the person making the offer) identifying terms of an agreement by which (s)he is prepared to be bound if they are accepted by the **offeree** (the person to whom the offer is made).

2. The consumer must distinguish between an offer and an 'invitation to treat' (for the different effects, see the diagram below):

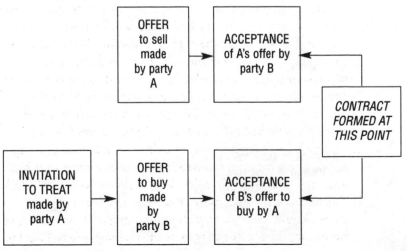

1. There are numerous examples of invitation to treat:
   - **Self-service shopping** – display of goods is the invitation to treat; a customer then selects goods and makes an offer to buy at the checkout which is then accepted or not by the shopkeeper (*Pharmaceutical Society of Great Britain v Boots Cash Chemists Ltd* (1953)).
   - The same applies to goods displayed in shop windows (*Fisher v Bell* (1961)) on whether display of a flick knife was unlawful under the Offensive Weapons Act.
   - **Advertisements** – the advertisement is the invitation to which a person responds by making an offer to buy (*Partridge v Crittenden* (1968)).
   - Mere **statement of price** – merely stating an acceptable price does not make it an offer to sell; the other party must still offer to buy at the price (*Harvey v Facey* (1893)).

2. In all cases the significance of the invitation to treat is that the person responding to it has not accepted an offer, so their action does not at that point create a binding contract.

3. Sometimes precise wording is more important than context. While something seems more like an invitation to treat it may in fact have the effect of an offer, so that a positive response by the other party may well lead to a contract being formed.

4. Precise wording may limit the people capable of responding to the offer, eg unilateral offers contained in advertisements, and otherwise seen as invitations to treat (*Carlill v Carbolic Smoke Ball Co.* (1893)) where the company offered £100 to anyone who used the smoke ball and still got flu and then tried to refuse to pay Mrs Carlill who complied with those conditions.

5. For an offer to be valid it must be **communicated** to the offeree. It would be unfair for a person be bound by an offer of which (s)he had no knowledge (*Taylor v Laird* (1856)).

6. An offer can be made to one individual, but also to the whole world, when the offer can be accepted by any party who had genuine notice of it (*Carlill v Carbolic Smoke Ball Co.* (1893)).

7. The terms of the offer must be certain. The parties must know in advance what they are contracting over. So any vague words may invalidate the agreement (*Guthing v Lynn* (1831)).

8. An offeror may withdraw the offer any time before the offeree has accepted it (*Routledge v Grant* (1828)). It would be unfair to expect the offeror to wait indefinitely for an offeree's response.

9. For an acceptance to be valid it must show an intention to be bound by the terms of the offer, so it must be unequivocal and unconditional, and correspond exactly with the terms of the offer – the 'mirror image' rule.

10. There can be no contract unless acceptance is communicated.

11. Only a genuine offeree can accept the offer, so an offer made without authority cannot be accepted (*Powell v Lee* (1908)).

12. It follows that silence cannot amount to an acceptance. (*Felthouse v Bindley* (1863)). An uncle wished to buy his nephew's horse. An auctioneer had sold the horse in error. The uncle's letter to the nephew that he would buy the horse if he heard no more was insufficient to show that a contract existed.

13. In some situations communication can be waived, eg unilateral contracts or through customary conduct between the parties.

14. Generally, acceptance can be in any form, but if a specific method of acceptance is known to be required then acceptance must be in that form in order to be valid. (*Compagnie de Commerce et Commissions SARL v Parkinson Stove Co.* (1953).)

2.1.3 Consideration

1. Contract law concerns enforcement of promises based on mutual agreement.

2. Consideration is the proof that the party seeking to enforce the contract was in fact a party to a mutual agreement by contributing something in return for the promise of the other party – so it is the *quid pro quo* – one thing in return for another.

3. So a consumer must show that he has given consideration in order to be able to enforce a contract.

4. The modern definition in *Dunlop v Selfridge* (1915) is to do with exchange; which repeats Sir Frederick Pollock's definition in *Principles of Contract*: 'An act of forbearance of one party, or the promise thereof, is the price for which the promise of the other is bought, and the promise thus given for value is enforceable'.
5. Consideration need not be 'adequate' in the ordinary sense – so a contract is enforceable even if the price does not match the value of what is being gained under the agreement (*Thomas v Thomas* (1842)).
6. But it must be 'sufficient' in a legal sense – it must be 'real, tangible, and have discernible value' (*Chappel v Nestlé* (1960)).
7. Only a person who has provided consideration under a contract can sue or be sued under the contract – so third parties who appear to have rights under the contract are nevertheless denied an action (*Tweddle v Atkinson* (1861)).
8. Although an exception to this is where third parties seek to enforce collateral warranties on which they have relied (*Shanklin Pier Ltd v Detel Products Ltd* (1951)).
9. And now, under the Contracts (Rights of Third Parties)) Act 1999, if third parties are identified in the contract as having the right to enforce it or in other circumstances where a third party is shown to have gained rights under the contract then they may enforce it – which can benefit people trying to return gifts that have been bought for them.

2.1.4 Intention to create legal relations

1. Contract law distinguishes between agreements needing the support of law and enforceable in the courts and entirely gratuitous promises or those where the law should not intervene.
2. The law has developed two rebuttable presumptions:
   - agreements that are purely domestic or social in nature are presumed not to be legally enforceable;
   - agreements in a business or commercial context are presumed to be legally binding unless the contrary is proved.

3. Giving free gifts may create legally enforceable arrangements if actually a disguised way of extending business (*McGowan v Radio Buxton* (2001)).

4. But it is possible expressly to exclude the possibility of legal enforceability within the agreement itself (*Jones v Vernons Pools* (1938)). The pools company did not have to pay out on a lost coupon because the coupon clearly stated that it was binding in honour only.

2.2 THE TERMS OF CONTRACTS

2.2.1 Terms and representations

1. Before formation, parties identify the basis on which they wish to contract.

2. Any statement of fact made at this stage is a 'representation'.

3. A term is a representation which is either expressly incorporated into the contract or implied by fact or by law.

4. So the consumer must distinguish terms from other representations, as terms form part of the contract and can be relied on.

5. Representations are of more or less significance to the parties.

6. The types of representation must be distinguished because the existence and character of liability depends on the type.

Type	If liability is created	Reason
Terms	Create binding obligations so attach liability (and range of remedies if breached))	Actually incorporated into the contract and so are the obligations under it
Mere representations	Attach no liability in themselves if correctly stated	They induce a party to enter a contract but do not become part of it – so not binding
Misrepresentations	Can attach liability (and range of remedies depending on how they are made – compare *Derry v Peek* with *Howard Marine & Dredging Co. v Ogden*)	Even though not part of the contract the representation did act to induce the other party to enter the contract and so vitiated their free will
Mere opinions	Attach no liability in themselves (*Bisset v Wilkinson*)	Opinion is not a matter of fact and is variable
Expert opinions	Can attach liability (as terms if important enough to be incorporated or as misrepresentations if falsely stated *Esso v Marden*)	Because we are entitled to rely and do rely on the skill and expertise of experts
Trade puffs	Attach no liability	Mere advertising boasts so we are deemed not to take them seriously
Puffs with an attached promise	May attach liability (*Carlill v The Carbolic Smoke Ball Co.*)	Because, although made in connection with a mere puff, the promise is sufficiently specific to be relied upon

Table illustrating consequences of different types of representation

Incorporating express terms:
A representation is only binding if incorporated as an express term of the contract
Incorporation is likely where:
- the representation is identified as important to one party (*Birch v Paramount Estates*);
- one party relies on the expertise of the other party (*Dick Bentley v Harold Smith Motors*);
- the statement and the making of the contract are close in time (*Routledge v McKay*);
- the contract is in writing;
- the contract is signed (*L'Estrange v Graucob*).

Implied terms:
Terms can be implied by fact, eg:
- by custom (*Hutton v Warren*);
- or by past dealings (*Hillas v Arcos*);
- or to make sense of the agreement (*Schawel v Reade*);
- or for commercial efficacy (*The Moorcock*).

This is based on the presumed intention of the parties – measured by the 'officious bystander' test in *Shirlaw v Southern Foundries*.
Terms can also be implied by statute, eg:
- Sale of Goods Act 1979;
- Supply of Goods and Services Act 1982.

TERMS

Construction of terms:
- Implied terms are construed according to how they are described.
- With express terms if the type of term is identified the judges usually give effect to the expressed intent of the parties.
- But the term must be accurately described (*Schuler v Wickman*).

If the contract is silent on the type of term then judges try to construe the intent of the parties.

The relative significance of terms:
- Terms can be of two types:
  - **conditions** – 'go to the root of the contract', so on breach have remedies available of repudiation and/or sue for damages (*Poussard v Spiers*);
  - **warranties** – generally descriptive terms, so only remedy on breach is to sue for damages (*Bettini v Gye*).
- Now there is also the innominate term – look for seriousness of breach (*Hong Kong Fir Shipping v Kawasaki Kisen Kaisha*).
- Very appropriate in the case of technical breaches (*Reardon Smith Line v Hansen Tangen*).

2.2.2 The nature of terms

1. A consumer will need to know the terms of the contract.
2. Terms are binding obligations which the parties agree to perform in order for the contract to be complete.
3. If either party fails to comply with the obligations they have set themselves there is breach of contract and potential legal action.
4. Terms can be:
   - expressly stated and incorporated into the contract;
   - implied factually from the circumstances as being the presumed intention of the parties;
   - imputed into the contract by process of law for some other purpose, eg for consumer protection.

2.2.3 Incorporating express terms into the contract

1. Not all representations become terms of the contract.
2. If the contract is written it is easier to determine which is a term.
3. The courts have devised tests to determine whether or not oral representations are incorporated into the contract as terms.
4. If not, may still be actionable misrepresentation if falsely stated.
5. Many factors can be taken into account in testing incorporation:
   - the importance attached to the representation by one party – the greater the importance attached, the more likely it is to be a term (*Birch v Paramount Estates* (1956));
   - the level of expertise of the representor: if one party relies on the other party's skill and judgment then it is likely to be a term (*Dick Bentley Productions Ltd v Harold Smith (Motors)) Ltd* (1965)) but a representation made without skill or expertise is less likely to be a term (*Oscar Chess Ltd*

v Williams (1957)). A person trading in a car could not be liable for representing the age of the car to the buyer when it was the age stated in the registration documents;

- the time span between the representation and formation of the contract – a longer gap and the representation is unlikely to be seen as a term (*Routledge v McKay*);
- whether a written agreement was signed – parties are taken to agree to everything they sign regardless of whether or not they have read it (*L'Estrange v Graucob* (1934));
- a representation will not become a term unless the party subject to it was aware of it at the time of contracting (*Olley v Marlborough Court Hotel Ltd* (1949)).

2.2.4 The process of implying terms into a contract

Contracting parties are deemed to include all the terms they wish to be bound by, but sometimes terms are implied:

- where in a dispute the court is trying to give effect to the presumed though unexpressed intentions of the parties – these are called terms implied by **fact**;
- where the law demands that certain provisions are included in a contract irrespective of the wishes of the parties – these are called terms implied by **law**.

2.2.5 Terms implied by fact

1. Courts imply terms into a contract for various reasons, including:
   - custom (*Hutton v Warren* (1836));
   - trade practice
   - to make sense of the agreement (*Schawel v Reade* (1913));
   - to follow prior conduct of parties (*Hillas v Arcos* (1932));
   - to preserve 'business efficacy' (*The Moorcock* (1889)).
2. The test of terms implied by fact is the 'officious bystander test' of MacKinnon LJ in *Shirlaw v Southern Foundries Ltd*

(1939) – 'prima facie that which is left to be implied is something so obvious that it goes without saying; so that, if while the parties were making their bargain, an officious bystander were to suggest some express provision they would testily suppress him with a common "Oh of course!"'.

3. In *Liverpool City Council v Irwin* (1976) Lord Denning said that the appropriate test was merely what was reasonable as between the parties. Lord Cross said it was what was necessary.

2.2.6 Terms implied by common law

1. On occasions judges will imply a term to regulate a particular type of agreement, irrespective of the wishes of the parties

2. They will do so because of the absence of statutory control of the area (*Liverpool City Council v Irwin* (1976)). A council was fixed with responsibility for maintaining common areas in flats even though this was not in the tenancy agreement.

3. Then the term will stand for future agreements of the same type, unless there is subsequent statutory intervention.

2.2.7 Terms implied by statute

1. Terms are implied by statute where government chooses to regulate certain types of agreements in order to protect weaker parties

2. Terms are implied to redress inequality of bargaining strength.

3. Such terms are enforceable whatever the wishes of the parties.

4. Examples are contracts of employment and consumer contracts.

5. In the Sale of Goods Act 1979 consumers are protected by the insertion of implied conditions in ss12, 13, 14(2), 14(3) and 15 (see Chapter 3).

6. In the Supply of Goods and Services Act 1982 consumers are protected by similar terms in ss3, 4 and 5 and by implied conditions in ss13, 14 and 15 (see Chapter 6).

2.2.8 The relative significance of terms

1. Inevitably, certain terms are more significant to the contract than others, some being fundamental to the purpose of the contract while others are merely ancillary to the main purpose.
2. The courts have traditionally distinguished them in two ways:
   - their significance to satisfactory completion of the contract;
   - the available remedy or remedies if the term is breached.
3. On this basis the courts have identified two types of term:
   - **conditions** –terms that 'go to the root of the contract', and are so fundamental that breach of the term would render the contract meaningless, so both an action for damages and/or repudiation is possible (*Poussard v Spiers and Pond* (1876));
   - **warranties** – minor/ancillary terms and their breach would not destroy purpose of the contract itself, so the available remedy is an action for damages only (*Bettini v Gye* (1876)).
4. Statutory implied terms are identified as one or the other in the Act, eg those in Sale of Goods Act 1979 are all stated as conditions.
5. Judges have rejected this strict categorisation in developing the concept of the 'innominate term':
   - aims for the remedy to be fair to both parties;
   - in *Hong Kong Fir Shipping Co Ltd v Kawasaki Kisen Kaisha Ltd* Lord Diplock said 'some breaches will, and others will not, give rise to an event which will deprive the party not in default of substantially the benefit he was intended to obtain from his contract', the remedy given would 'depend on the nature of the event to which the breach gives rise';
   - so the court should wait and see what the consequences of the breach are in deciding a remedy (*Cehave NV v Bremer Handelsgesellschaft dbH (The Hansa Nord))* (1976));

- calling terms 'innominate' is effective if the breach is purely technical (*Reardon Smith Line v Hansen Tangen* (1976));

6. But courts may refuse to classify terms as conditions, whatever the consequences of the breach when circumstances demand (*Bunge Corporation v Tradex Export Panama* (1980)).

2.2.9 How judges construe terms

1. Where the contract states that a term is a condition or warranty then it is generally as simple as following that classification.

2. However, if the contract is silent the judges will need to construe which classification is appropriate, which they do as follows:
   - in the case of a statutory implied term, judges follow the standards set by the law;
   - in the case of an express term, where the parties have already classified the term the judges will generally give effect to the expressed intention of the parties;
   - in the case of express terms which are silent on their classification, judges will try to give effect what they believe is the intention of the parties.

3. However, express classification may be inaccurate since a party can gain advantage by calling every term a condition. In this case judges will construe the term according to how it really operates (*Schuler v Wickman Machine Tool Sales Ltd* (1973)).

4. In deciding a classification they may use the commercial context of the agreement as a guide (*Meredelanto Compania Naviera SA v Bergbau-Handel GmbH (The Mihalis Angelos))* (1970)).

Misrepresentation defined:

- A falsely made statement of material fact (not opinion (*Bisset v Wilkinson*) nor future intention (*Edgington v Fitzmaurice*) nor trade puffs (*Carlill v Carbolic Smoke Ball Co.*).
- Made by one party to the other party (not by a third party) (*Peyman v Lanjani*).
- Before formation, not after (*Roscorla v Thomas*).
- Intended to induce the other party to enter the contract.
- But not to form part of it.

Classes of misrepresentation and remedies:

Fraudulent misrepresentation:
- brought under the tort of deceit;
- must be made deliberately or knowingly, without belief in truth, or carelessly (*Derry v Peek*);
- so defence merely = honest belief.

Remedies =
- sue for damages, under tort measure, including all consequential loss (*Smith New Court Securities v Scrimgeour*);
- affirm contract, or disaffirm and use as defence to claim of breach or seek rescission in equity.

Negligent misrepresentation:
- sue in tort under *Hedley Byrne* where there is a 'special relationship';
- sue under s2(1) Misrepresentation Act (*Howard Marine Dredging v Ogden*);
- remedy = damages (tort measure).

Innocent misrepresentation:
- sue under s2(2) for damages or seek rescission.

MISREPRESENTATION

Non-disclosure:

No basic common law duty to disclose information not requested (*Fletcher v Krell*).

But exceptions are:
- *uberrimae fides* (utmost good faith) (*Locker & Woolf v Western Australian Insurance Co*);
- part truth (*Dimmock v Hallett*);
- true statement becomes false (*With v O'Flannagan*).

Equity and misrepresentation:

Contract voidable, not void, so rescission possible if:
- *restitutio in integrum* possible (*Lagunas Nitrate v Lagunas Syndicate*);
- contract not affirmed (*Long v Lloyd*);
- no excessive delay (*Leaf v International Galleries*);
- no third party rights gained (*Car & Universal Finance v Caldwell*).

Indemnity is also possible (*Whittington v Seale-Hayne*).

2.3 MISREPRESENTATION

2.3.1 Introduction

1. If a consumer cannot show breach of a term because the representation was not incorporated as part of the contract, he may still have an action for misrepresentation.
2. The 'representations' made prior to formation can become terms if incorporated or will remain outside of the contract.
3. 'Mere representations' have no contractual significance. They are used to induce the other party to enter the contract, but if accurately stated create no liability.
4. Only a falsely stated or inaccurate representation is actionable.
5. The motive behind the falsehood is not vital to establishing that a misrepresentation exists, but it can be important in deciding the class of misrepresentation, and the remedies available.
6. If misrepresentation is established, the contract is voidable, and the victim of the misrepresentation may avoid his obligations under the contract or have the contract set aside.
7. There are many practical considerations to remember:
   - traditionally there were virtually no remedies available so it was vital to prove that that the false representation was incorporated as a term. It may still be beneficial to do so;
   - misrepresentation is a fairly new class of action created in statute although there are some limited common law possibilities either through tort or in equity;
   - misrepresentation is close in character to common mistake. The latter is sometimes preferred because a successful claim makes the contract void rather than voidable.

2.3.2 Misrepresentation defined

1. A misrepresentation is:
- a statement of material fact;
- made by one party to a contract to the other party;
- before or at the time of formation of the contract;
- which was intended to act as an inducement to the other party to enter the contract and was such an inducement;
- but was not intended as a binding obligation of the contract;
- and which was falsely or incorrectly stated.

2. If any of these requirements is not present then, whatever else it is, the representation complained of is not a misrepresentation.

3. A statement of material fact must not be:
- a mere opinion (unless it was not actually held) (*Bisset v Wilkinson* (1927)) – a statement in the sale of land of how many sheep it would hold was not actionable as the seller had no experience of sheep farming; or
- an expression of future intent (unless it falsely represents a current state of mind) (*Edgington v Fitzmaurice* (1885)); or
- a mere trade puff (on the maxim *simplex commendatio non obligat*): (*Carlill v The Carbolic Smoke Ball Co.* (1893)).

4. Anything said by a third party (except an agent of a party) cannot be a misrepresentation (*Peyman v Lanjani* (1985)).

5. A statement made after formation is not actionable (*Roscorla v Thomas* (1842)).

6. To be an inducement to the other party:
- the representation must be materially important to the making of the contract (*JEB Fasteners Ltd v Mark Bloom & Co.* (1983));
- And the party must actually be induced (*Museprime Properties Ltd v Adhill Properties Ltd* (1990)).

To be an inducement, the representation must not:
- remain unknown to the other party;
- already be known as false by the other party;

- neither be believed or relied upon (*Attwood v Small* (1838)).
7. If intended to be binding it is likely to be a breach of warranty rather than a misrepresentation (*Couchman v Hill* (1947)).
8. If the representation is accurate then the contract is complete.

2.3.3 Classes of misrepresentation and their remedies

1. Misrepresentation can vary from telling deliberate lies to innocently repeating inaccurate information.
2. Originally, with no remedy available for misrepresentation, it was vital to prove incorporation and thus breach of a term
3. Prior to the Misrepresentations Act 1967 there was some development in tort and in equity, but not really in contract law itself.
4. This meant that the significance of the class of misrepresentation was in how it could be proved and what remedy was available
5. The significance lessened after the 1967 Act.

2.3.4 Fraudulent misrepresentation

1. Originally the only available common-law action.
2. Brought under the tort of deceit and available only where fraud can be proved.
3. Fraud was defined in *Derry v Peek* (1889) by Lord Herschell as where the false representation was made either:
   - knowingly or deliberately; or
   - without belief in its truth; or
   - reckless, without caring whether it was true or not.
4. So the best defence is to show an honest belief:
   - which need not be reasonable, merely honestly held;
   - so fraud is very hard to prove.
5. The motive for fraud is irrelevant (*Akerhielm v De Mare* (1959)).

6. Recklessness is only evidence of fraud, not proof, unless it amounts to blatant disregard for the truth and so is also dishonest (*Thomas Witter Ltd v TBP Industries Ltd* (1996)).

2.3.5 The remedies for fraudulent misrepresentation

1. By suing in the tort of deceit, the measure of damages is in tort.
2. The test of damages is now in *Smith New Court Securities Ltd. v Scrimgeour Vickers (Asset Management) Ltd* (1996):
   - the defendant is responsible for all damages, including any consequential loss, provided that there is a causal link between the misrepresentation and damage;
   - this results in heavier claims and so encourages fraud actions.
3. Where suing for damages the claimant can also:
   - affirm the contract and continue with it; or
   - disaffirm the contract and refuse any further performance.
4. Two other possibilities if the claimant refuses further performance:
   - take no action, if no advantage is to be gained, but use the fraud as a defence to the other party's counterclaim (and the claimant may refuse to return, eg insurance premiums paid);
   - seek rescission of the contract in equity.

2.3.6 Negligent misrepresentation

1. Traditionally, all non-fraudulent misrepresentations were classed as innocent, with no action or remedy available at common law.
2. Now actions are available both at common law and by statute.
3. At common law:
   - an action for negligent mis-statement causing a financial loss, established in *Hedley Byrne v Heller & Partners* (1964);

- liability arises only if the representor owes a duty of care to the representee, so a 'special relationship' must exist;
- and the appropriate test for liability requires:
  - possession of a particular type of knowledge by the defendant (*Harris v Wyre Forest DC* (1988));
  - proximity between the parties (not necessarily contractual) (*Caparo Industries v Dickman* (1990));
  - the defendant is aware that the claimant is relying on the advice given (*Chaudhry v Prabhakar* (1988));
- the principle may also cover representations as to a future state of affairs (*Esso Petroleum Co. Ltd v Marden* (1976)).

4. By statute:
- statutory liability is in s2(1) Misrepresentation Act 1967
  - if as a result of a misrepresentation a person has suffered loss then the person making it is liable for damages even though it was not made fraudulently, unless he can show he had reasonable grounds to believe in the statement;
- there are a number of consequences to the Act:
  - the burden of proof is reversed;
  - the claimant can choose to claim under the Act or common law;
  - there is no need to show a special relationship under the Act (*Howard Marine Dredging Co. Ltd v A Ogden & Sons (Excavating) Ltd* (1978)).

2.3.7 Remedies for negligent misrepresentation

1. Damages are available both under the Act and at common law.
2. At common law the measure is that for tort, based on foreseeable loss.
3. The Act uses a tort measure but it is uncertain whether it is that in the tort of deceit (*Royscott Trust Ltd v Rogerson* (1991)).
4. Damages can be reduced for contributory negligence.
5. Traditionally, all non-fraudulent misrepresentation was classed as innocent and the only remedy would be rescission in equity.

2.3.8 Innocent misrepresentation

1. Innocent representation after the Act probably only refers to repeating inaccurate information, honestly believing it to be true.
2. No common law action but rescission always possible in equity.
3. Now, if s2(1) is not available, there is the possibility of damages under s2(2) as an alternative to rescission.

2.3.9 Remedies for innocent misrepresentation

1. Since damages would not be available at common law, they are not available under s2(1) either.
2. But damages are available under s2(2) if rescission is possible.
3. So four points can be made:
   - there is no absolute, only a discretionary, right to damages;
   - damages are instead of, not as well as, rescission;
   - the measure of damages is uncertain;
   - an innocent misrepresentation may be incorporated which may give claimant rights as terms (*Watts v Spence* (1975)).
4. Rescission, the only former remedy, was granted because 'no man ought to be able to take advantage of his own false statements' – Sir George Jessel in (*Redgrave v Hurd* (1881)).

2.3.10 Equity and misrepresentation

1. An actionable misrepresentation makes the contract voidable, not void, so the contract is valid until set aside by one party.
2. Rescission is available whatever class of misrepresentation but:
   - it is a discretionary remedy; and
   - the court must consider the degree of seriousness of the breach and the likely consequences of rescission.
3. The right to rescind may be lost in certain circumstances:
   - if *restitutio in integrum* is impossible (if the parties cannot be restored to their pre-contractual position) (*Lagunas*

Nitrate Co. v Lagunas Syndicate (1899)).
- if the contract is affirmed (*Long v Lloyd* (1958));
- excessive delay (*Leaf v International Galleries* (1950));
- if a third party has gained rights in the property (*Car and Universal Finance Co. Ltd v Caldwell* (1964));
- if under s2(2) the court feels that damages is the more appropriate remedy.

4. It is possible to recover an indemnity at the same time as rescission (*Whittington v Seale-Hayne* (1900)).

2.3.11 Non-disclosure amounting to misrepresentation

1. There is no basic common-law obligation to disclose information not requested by the other party (*Fletcher v Krell* (1873)).

2. So silence on its own need not be misrepresentation (*Hands v Simpson, Fawcett & Co.* (1928)).

3. Sometimes, however, withholding of information is actionable:
- in contracts *uberrimae fides* (those where the utmost good faith is required) (*Locker and Woolf v Western Australian Insurance Co.* (1936)), eg in contracts of insurance;
- in contracts involving fiduciary relationships (*Tate v Williamson* (1866));
- where part-truth amounts to falsehood (*Dimmock v Hallett* (1866));
- where a true statement becomes false during the negotiations and the other side is not informed (*With v O'Flannagan* (1936)).

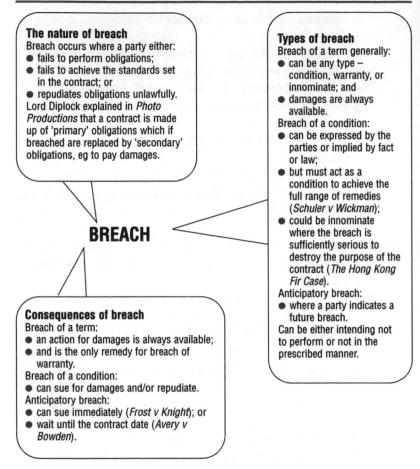

The nature of breach
Breach occurs where a party either:
- fails to perform obligations;
- fails to achieve the standards set in the contract; or
- repudiates obligations unlawfully.

Lord Diplock explained in *Photo Productions* that a contract is made up of 'primary' obligations which if breached are replaced by 'secondary' obligations, eg to pay damages.

Types of breach
Breach of a term generally:
- can be any type – condition, warranty, or innominate; and
- damages are always available.

Breach of a condition:
- can be expressed by the parties or implied by fact or law;
- but must act as a condition to achieve the full range of remedies (*Schuler v Wickman*);
- could be innominate where the breach is sufficiently serious to destroy the purpose of the contract (*The Hong Kong Fir Case*).

Anticipatory breach:
- where a party indicates a future breach.

Can be either intending not to perform or not in the prescribed manner.

BREACH

Consequences of breach
Breach of a term:
- an action for damages is always available;
- and is the only remedy for breach of warranty.

Breach of a condition:
- can sue for damages and/or repudiate.

Anticipatory breach:
- can sue immediately (*Frost v Knight*); or
- wait until the contract date (*Avery v Bowden*).

2.4 BREACH OF CONTRACT

2.4.1 The nature of a breach of contract

1. A breach occurs if a party fails to perform contractual obligations.

2. This can occur in one of three ways:
- failure to perform an obligation;

- failure to match the quality of performance required by the contract;
- repudiating obligations unlawfully, ie without justification.

3. Calling failure to perform obligations a discharge of them seems somewhat illogical – Lord Diplock explained the position in *Photo Productions Ltd v Securicor Transport Ltd* (1980):
   - the original contractual obligations are **primary** obligations;
   - on breach these obligations are replaced (rather than discharged)) by **secondary** obligations, eg to pay damages.

4. He also identified two basic exceptions to this rule:
   - **'fundamental breach'** – if a party breaches a fundamental term (one depriving the other party of the major benefit they expected under the contract), the whole contract is breached;
   - **breach of a condition** – where the term is so central to the contract that failure to perform makes it meaningless.

5. The difference between these two traditionally was that an exclusion clause could not be relied upon in a fundamental breach but exclusion of liability for a condition could succeed.

2.4.2 The different types of breach

1. There are three identifiable types of breach:
2. Breach of a term generally:
   - here, it does not matter how the term is classified; and
   - it might include a minor breach of an innominate term;
   - on breach an action for damages is always available.
3. Breach of a condition:
   - a condition can either be expressed by the parties or implied by fact or law;
   - to produce the full range of remedies it must, however, conform to the proper description of a condition (*Schuler v Wickman Machine Tool Sales Ltd* (1973));

- it might also include an innominate term where the breach was sufficiently serious to warrant repudiation by the other party (*The Hong Kong Fir case* (1962));
- and fundamental breach if it survived the *Securicor* cases.

4. Anticipatory breach:
   - occurs if one party expressly or impliedly notifies the other party of intention to breach the contract – so more accurately described as breach by anticipatory repudiation (*Hoechster v De La Tour* (1853)). Under the contract Hoechster was due to begin work as a courier two months from the contract date. The defendant then cancelled the contract a month before it was due to start, and his argument that the claimant needed to wait till he was due to commence work failed;
   - not all terms need to be breached, and it may merely refer to performance other than in the prescribed manner.

2.4.3 The consequences of breach

1. The consequences of breach can vary with the type of breach.
2. Breach of a term generally:
   - an action for damages is always available;
   - with a warranty only an action for damages is available and any attempt to repudiate obligations will be a breach.
3. Breach of a condition:
   - the party can sue and/or repudiate obligations;
   - before repudiating the party must be sure that the term is a condition or there is a sufficiently serious breach, otherwise that repudiation may itself be a breach (*Cehave NV v Bremen Handelsgesellschaft mbH (The Hansa Nord)* (1975)).
4. Anticipatory breach:
   - here, the victim of the breach may treat the contract as at an end and sue immediately (*Frost v Knight* (1872));
   - alternatively, the party may wait until performance is actually due and remains unperformed (*Avery v Bowden*

(1855)). When it became clear that Bowden was unable to meet his contractual obligation to load cargo, Avery was able to wait until the obligation was due, to be able sue. This was a mistake as war frustrated the contract in the meantime;

- however, this may leave that party without a remedy if (s)he becomes liable for a later breach (*Fercometal SARL v Mediterranean Shipping Co. SA* (1988));
- An anticipatory breach can also arise if a party mistakenly treats an anticipatory breach as an actual breach and then treats the contract as having ended (*Federal Commerce and Navigation Co. Ltd v Molena Alpha Inc.* (1979)).

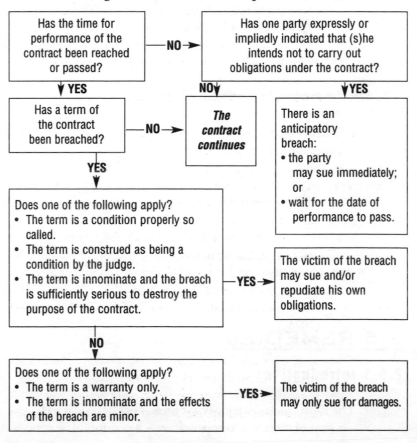

Causation and remoteness of damage:
- Breach must be the main reason for the claimant's loss (*London Joint Stock Bank v MacMillan*).
- Two types of loss for which the claimant can recover – (i) natural consequence of the breach; (ii) that in the contemplation of parties at time contract formed (*Hadley v Baxendale*).
- Based on what is foreseeable (*Victoria Laundry v Newman*).

Bases of assessment:
Three normal bases:
- **loss of a bargain** – eg loss of profit, or failure to the 'available market' rule – compare *Charter v Sullivan* and *Thompson v Robinson Gunmakers*;
- **reliance loss**, ie necessary expenses made in advance of contract (*Anglia TV v Reed*);
- **restitution**, ie a price already paid under the contract.

DAMAGES

Liquidated damages:
Identified in the contract itself
Must not be a penalty
Test in *Dunlop v New Garage*:
- extravagant sum is a penalty;
- payment of a large sum for a small debt is a penalty;
- one sum for a variety of breaches is a penalty; a sum for one breach is not;
- wording used by parties not conclusive, but construction by court;
- a claim for liquidated damages will not fail because potential loss was impossible to calculate at the time of formulation.

Mental distress:
Possible for claimant and his/her family in holiday cases (*Jarvis v Swan Tours* and *Jackson v Horizon Holidays*).

2.5 REMEDIES

2.5.1 Introduction

1. The most common remedy for breach of contract is damages – a sum of money in compensation – a common-law remedy.

2. It is artificial and nothing to do with enforcing the contract – as a result of its shortcomings, other remedies developed in equity.

3. If a case is proven at common law, damages are automatically granted – equitable remedies are at the discretion of the court.

4. While a claimant must state in the pleadings which remedy is required, both types of remedy can be granted at the same time.

5. Two types of compensation available at common law:
- a sum of unliquidated damages based on the precise loss;
- a liquidated sum – this is fixed by the parties when the contract was formed.

2.5.2 Unliquidated damages

1. Contract damages are to 'put the victim of the breach, so far as is possible and so far as the law allows, into the position he would have been in if the contract had not been broken': Parke B in *Robinson v Harman* (1848).

2. Nominal damages are possible even if no actual loss is suffered.

3. There are two tests establishing exactly what a party will recover:
- one to determine the type of loss for which the claimant can recover – based on causation and remoteness of damage;
- one to establish the amount recoverable in respect of the actual loss – called the bases of assessment.

2.5.3 Tests of causation and remoteness of damage

1. Here there are two key questions:
- is there a causal link between the defendant's breach and the actual damage or loss suffered by the claimant?;
- is the damage of a type that is not too remote a consequence of the defendant's breach?

2. Causation:

- Causation is a question of fact in each case – the court decides if the breach is the main reason for the claimant's loss (*London Joint Stock Bank v MacMillan* (1918)).

- The test is a common-sense one of whether the breach was the cause or merely the occasion of the loss (*Galoo Ltd and Others v Bright Grahame Murray* (1995)).

- The loss may be the result of the character of the contract itself rather than any breach, in which case the defendant is not liable (*C & P Haulage v Middleton* (1983)).

- The loss may arise partly from the breach and partly from an intervening event (*Stansbie v Troman* (1948): a decorator contracted to lock up left premises unlocked, allowing burglars easy access and thus helping to cause the loss).

- In which case the chain of causation is not broken if it is a reasonably foreseeable event (*De La Bere v Pearson* (1908)).

- If there are two causal factors including the breach then the loss can still be attributed to the breach (*Smith, Hogg & Co. v Black Sea Insurance* (1940)).

3. Remoteness of damage:

- Alderson B said that damages should be for losses 'such as may fairly and reasonably be considered arising either naturally i.e. according to the usual course of things, for such breach of contract itself, or such as may be reasonably supposed to have been in the contemplation of both parties at the time they made the contract.' (*Hadley v Baxendale* (1854) where carriers, in breach of contract, failed to deliver a crankshaft to a mill at the time specified, causing lost profit.)

- So there are two possible types of recoverable loss:
  - a natural consequence of the breach – measured **objectively**;
  - a loss which, if not a natural consequence, the parties knew was possible when they contracted – measured **subjectively**.

- Since modified by Asquith LJ in *Victoria Laundry Ltd v Newman Industries Ltd* (1949)). A boiler was ordered and delivered after the due date. Suppliers were liable for normal loss of profits but not loss of a lucrative government contract of which they were unaware. The judgment has six vital points:
  - to indemnify any loss is too harsh on the defendant;
  - recoverable loss should be measured against foreseeability;
  - foresight depends on the knowledge of the parties when contracting;
  - knowledge is of two types: (i) imputed knowledge, ie common knowledge; and (ii) actual knowledge, ie that actually possessed by the parties on formation of the contract (these two types represent the two identified in *Hadley v Baxendale*);
  - but knowledge can also be implied from what a reasonable man might have contemplated;
  - implied knowledge should include what it is possible to have foreseen rather than what must have been foreseen.
- The test can cause confusion. The House of Lords added to the confusion in *Koufos v C Czarnikow Ltd (The Heron II)* (1969) where they held: (i) often the reasonable man ought to contemplate certain loss as a natural consequence of a breach; and (ii) foresight is different in contract and tort. Here, the loss was recoverable when a sugar cargo was late arriving in a trading port and the sugar was for resale.
- This was rejected by the Court of Appeal in *H Parsons (Livestock)) Ltd v Uttley Ingham* (1978) holding that remoteness is not dependent on contemplation of possible level of injury but merely proof that loss could be contemplated.

2.5.4 The bases of assessment

1. If no loss is suffered but a breach is proved, eg to declare a contract ended, then nominal damages can be granted (*Staniforth v Lyall* (1830)).

2. There are 3 normal bases of assessment:
- Loss of a bargain – which puts the party in the position as if the contract had been properly performed; it includes:
  - where goods or services are defective, the difference between the contract quality and the quality received (*Bence Graphics International Ltd v Fasson UK Ltd* (1996));
  - in a failure to deliver goods or a refusal to accept delivery the difference between the contract price and that in an 'available market', ie if the claimant can get the goods or sell the goods for the same price or even make a better bargain then there is no entitlement to damages (*Charter v Sullivan* (1957)), but if the claimant must pay more to get the goods or cannot get rid of the goods because there is no available market then recovery is possible (*W L Thompson Ltd v Robinson Gunmakers Ltd* (1955));
  - loss of profit;
  - loss of a chance (*Chaplin v Hicks* (1911)): an actress recovered in respect of an audition she was prevented from attending when 50 people were to audition. But not if the claimant just takes advantage of the defendant's breach (*Pilkington v Wood* (1953)).
- Reliance loss:
  - recovery of the expenses that the claimant has necessarily incurred in advance of the contract being performed;
  - which is normally claimed when any loss of profit is too speculative (*Anglia Television v Reed* (1972));
  - usually impossible to recover both loss of a bargain and reliance loss since it is compensating twice for the same loss;

– but it may if the loss of a bargain claim covers only net rather than gross profit (*Western Web Offset Printers Ltd v Independent Media Ltd* (1995)).

- Restitution:
  – this is a simple repayment of any of the price already paid over by the claimant.

2.5.5 The duty to mitigate

1. A claimant has a duty to take 'all reasonable steps to mitigate the loss consequent on the breach' which then 'debars him from claiming in respect of any part of the damage which is due to his neglect to take such steps': Lord Haldane in *British Westinghouse Electric and Manufacturing Co. Ltd v Underground Electric Railways Co. of London Ltd* (1912)).
2. The claimant must not take any unreasonable steps that would increase the loss (*The Borag* (1981)).
3. However, the claimant is not bound to take extraordinary steps to mitigate the loss (*Pilkington v Wood* (1953)).
4. In an anticipatory breach the claimant need not terminate at once to mitigate the loss, but can wait until the actual breach (*White and Carter v McGregor* (1962)).

2.5.6 The 'mental distress' cases

1. Traditionally, judges would not allow recovery of compensation that would be more appropriately claimed in a tort action:
   - so, a claim for injury to reputation and consequent mental distress failed in *Addis v The Gramophone Co.* (1909));
   - as did a claim for indignity (*Hurst v Picture Theatres* (1913)).
2. More recently, judges have given damages for mental distress in certain limited circumstances in the so-called 'holiday cases':
   - loss of enjoyment and inconvenience caused by double booking (*Cook v Spanish Holidays* (1960));

- mental distress caused by a total failure to match the description given (*Jarvis v Swan Tours* (1973)). A so-called 'Tyrolean' holiday had few of the features in the brochure;
- mental distress caused to the claimant's family (despite inconsistency with privity) (*Jackson v Horizon Holidays* (1975) in which Lord Denning explained that the basis of the claim is that 'the provision of comfort, pleasure, and "peace of mind" was a central feature of the contract').

3. The principle only applies to the holiday cases and is not appropriate to commercial contracts (*Woodar Investment Development Ltd v Wimpey Construction UK Ltd* (1980)).
4. More recently, damages have been awarded for 'loss of amenity' where the sole purpose of the contract was 'the provision of a pleasurable amenity' (*Ruxley Electronics and Construction Ltd v Forsyth: Laddingford Enclosures Ltd v Forsyth* (1995)).

2.5.7 Liquidated damage clauses

1. These apply where parties fix in advance in the contract the sum of damages payable in the event of a breach.
2. The court will only enforce the sum identified where it represents a proper assessment of the loss.
3. There are two possibilities:
   - the sum fixed in the contract is declared valid and no further claim for unliquidated damages is then possible;
   - the sum in the contract is seen as a 'penalty', ie it does not relate to the actual loss – in this case a claim for unliquidated damages is possible.
4. Wherever a clause provides for a greater sum than the actual loss it is *prima facie* void and the party claiming it must prove that it is not a penalty in order to succeed in the claim (*Bridge v Campbell Discount Co.* (1962)).
5. In *Dunlop Pneumatic Tyre Co. v New Garage & Motor Co.* (1914) Lord Dunedin established a test for differentiating between genuine liquidated damages and penalties:

- an extravagant sum is generally a penalty;
- payment of a large sum for default on a small debt is most likely a penalty;
- one sum operating for a variety of breaches is likely to be a penalty, whereas a sum that relates to a single breach is not;
- the wording used by the parties is not conclusive – it is the construction by the court that counts;
- a claim for liquidated damages will not fail because potential loss was impossible to calculate at the time of formation.

CHAPTER 3

SALE OF GOODS

S12 right to sell:
- seller has right to sell;
- goods are free from any charge;
- buyer will enjoy quiet possession.

S13 goods will correspond to description:
- this section applies to private sales as well as business sales;
- there can be sale by description even if buyer selects goods;
- consumers can reject goods that do not match description;
- it is not a sale by description if the seller makes it clear that his judgement cannot be relied on.

TERMS IMPLIED BY THE SALE OF GOODS ACT 1979

S14 goods must be of satisfactory quality:
- the standard is what a reasonable person would regard as satisfactory;
- takes into account description of goods, price and other relevant circumstances;
- quality includes:
  - fitness for purpose;
  - appearance, finish;
  - freedom from minor defects;
  - safety and durability;
- fitness for purpose includes any purpose made known expressly or by implication.

S15 sale by sample:
- the bulk must match the sample;
- the bulk must be of satisfactory quality.

3.1 CONTRACTS WITHIN THE SALE OF GOODS ACT 1979

1. Section 2(1) of the Sale of Goods Act 1979 (SGA) defines a contract for the sale of goods as one under which 'the seller transfers or agrees to transfer property in goods to the buyer for a money consideration called the price'.
2. This includes credit sales and hire purchase contracts where there is an obligation to buy. (Hire purchase contracts where there is only an option to buy are protected under the Supply of Goods (Implied Terms) Act 1973.)
3. Free goods which are given in order to promote the sale of other goods are not included (*Esso Petroleum Co. v Commissioners of Custom and Excise* (1976)).
4. If the contract is predominantly for other purposes, eg services, it is not a contract for sale of goods, even though some goods may pass under it: eg a contract for a portrait to be painted.
5. To be a contract for services and not of goods, the value of the service must exceed the value of the goods (*Robinson v Graves* (1935)).
6. However, if it is predominantly a contract for services then terms will be implied into it under the Supply of Goods and Services Act 1982 (see Chapter 6).
7. Computer software has been held to be 'goods' within the SGA (*St Albans City and District Council v International Computers Ltd* (1996)).

3.2 TERMS IMPLIED BY THE SALE OF GOODS ACT 1979

1. Sections 12, 13, 14 and 15 of the 1979 Act imply terms into contracts for the sale of goods.
2. S12(1) implies that the seller has the right to sell and so will pass a good title to the buyer.

3. S12(2) implies that the goods are free from any charge or other encumbrance and that the buyer will be able to enjoy quiet possession of the goods.
4. S13 implies that goods will match their description (see section 3.3 below).
5. S14 implies that goods are of satisfactory quality (see section 3.4 below).
6. S15 implies that, where there is a sale by sample, the bulk of the goods will match the sample (see section 3.5 below).
7. S6 of the Unfair Contract Terms Act 1977 states that:
   - the implied terms under s12 can never be excluded from any contract (consumer or non-consumer);
   - the implied terms under ss13–15 cannot be excluded from consumer contracts.

3.3 IMPLIED TERMS ABOUT DESCRIPTION

1. Section 13(1) SGA states that 'Where there is a contract for the sale of goods by description there is an implied term that the goods will correspond with the description'.
2. If the sale is by sample, as well as by description, it is not sufficient that the bulk of the goods corresponds with the sample, if the goods do not also correspond with the description (s13(2)).
3. A sale of goods is not prevented from being a sale by description by reason only that, being exposed for sale or hire, they are selected by the buyer (s13(3)). This makes it a sale by description where, eg a shopper buys a pre-packed food with a list of ingredients on the packaging.
4. S13 applies to private sales as well as consumer sales: ie where the seller is not selling in the course of business (*Beale v Taylor* (1967)).
5. The section has been given a wide interpretation by the courts, as in *Beale v Taylor* (1967) where the words 'Herald convertible, white, 1961' in an advert were held to be a

description of the car.

6. It is not a sale by description if the seller makes it clear that his judgement cannot be relied on (*Harlingdon and Leinster Enterprises Ltd v Christopher Hull Fine Art Ltd* (1991)).

7. Where a term has acquired a special meaning then that meaning is used (*Grenfell v EB Meyrowitz Ltd* (1936)).

3.3.1 Rejection of goods

1. In the past, the buyer could always reject the goods if they did not match the description, even though the goods were fit for their purpose, as in *Re Moore & Co and Landauer & Co.* (1931) (description of the number of cans packed in each box).

2. There is a now a distinction between consumer contracts and non-consumer contracts.

3. A consumer can always reject goods which do not match their description.

4. However, in non-consumer contracts where the breach is so slight that it would be unreasonable for the buyer to reject the goods, then the breach is only of warranty (s15A) and the buyer cannot reject the goods.

3.4 IMPLIED TERMS ABOUT QUALITY AND FITNESS

1. There is a basic rule of *caveat emptor* which means 'let the buyer beware'. However, the law implies various terms about quality and fitness into contracts for the sale of goods.

2. Where the SGA does not apply then the rule *caveat emptor* still applies, as recognised by the SGA in s14(1) which states that 'Except as provided by this section … there is no implied condition or warranty about the quality or fitness for any particular purpose of goods supplied under a contract of sale'.

3. Section 14(2) states that 'Where the seller sells goods in the course of a business there is an implied terms that the goods supplied are of satisfactory quality'.

4. The sale of second-hand goods is covered by this section (*Crowther v Shannon Motor Co.* (1975)).

5. If there is a breach of the implied term, the seller is liable for any injuries or damage which is caused by the breach (*Godley v Perry* (1960): loss of an eye through faulty catapult).

3.4.1 Satisfactory quality

1. Prior to 1994 the test was whether the goods were of merchantable quality. This was replaced by the test of 'satisfactory quality'.

2. The need for change was highlighted by cases such as *Bernstein v Pamson Motors (Golders Green)* (1987) and *Rogers v Parish (Scarborough) Ltd* (1987) (problems with minor defects and finish).

3. The Law Commission made recommendations which led to the passing of the Sale of Goods (Amendment) Act 1994 amending the wording of the SGA 1979.

4. Now, under the SGA, goods are of satisfactory quality if they meet the standard that a reasonable person would regard as satisfactory, taking account of any description of the goods, the price (if relevant) and all other relevant circumstances (s14(2A)).

5. Section 14(2B) states that quality of the goods includes their state or condition and the following (among others) are in appropriate cases aspects of the quality of goods:
   (a) fitness for all the purposes for which goods of the kind in question are commonly supplied;
   (b) appearance and finish;
   (c) freedom from minor defects;
   (d) safety;
   (e) durability.

6. Under s14(2D) relevant circumstances include public statements made by the seller or producer in advertising or labelling.

7. There have been very few cases since 1994 to judge the meaning or the success of the new wording.

3.4.2 Excluded situations

1. The implied term of satisfactory quality does not extend to any matter making the quality unsatisfactory which is specifically drawn to the buyer's attention before the contract is made (s14(2C)).
2. S14(2C) also excludes situations where:
   - the buyer examines the goods before the contract is made and examination ought to reveal the defect; or
   - in the case of a contract for sale by sample, the defect would have been apparent on a reasonable examination of the sample.

3.4.3 Fitness for a particular purpose

1. Where the seller sells goods in the course of a business and the buyer, expressly or by implication, makes known any particular purpose for which the goods are being bought, there is an implied term that the goods supplied are reasonably fit for that purpose (s14(3)).
2. This is so whether or not the purpose is one for which such goods are commonly supplied.
3. The purpose may be made known by implication where the purpose of the goods is obvious, eg a hot-water bottle (*Preist v Last* (1903)) or a catapult (*Godley v Perry* (1960)).
4. Where the buyer makes known a specific purpose then the purpose is expressly stated, as in *St Albans City and District Council v International Computers Ltd* (1996) (use of computer software).
5. Where either the buyer does not rely on the skill or judgement of the seller or it would be unreasonable for him to do so there is no implied term, as in *Griffiths v Peter Conway Ltd* (1939) (fact of extra-sensitive skin not made known).

3.5 IMPLIED TERMS ABOUT SAMPLES

1. S15 SGA implies a term that, in a sale by sample, the bulk of the goods will match the sample.
2. This is of importance in consumer purchases of such goods as carpets or other furnishings where the choice is often made from a sample.

3.6 PASSING OF PROPERTY AND RISK

1. The rules are set out in s18 and apply to all sale of goods contract, consumer and non-consumer.
2. The main rule is that the property in the goods which are identified and agreed upon passes at the time the contract is made unless an agreement to the contrary is made (s18, rule 1).

3.7 ACCEPTANCE OF GOODS

1. It is important to know when the buyer is deemed to have accepted the goods as, at that point, the buyer loses his right to reject the goods (though he may still claim for damages).
2. The buyer is deemed to have accepted the goods when:
   - he intimates to the seller that he has accepted them; or
   - the goods have been delivered to him and he does any act in relation to them which is inconsistent with the ownership of the seller (s35(1)).
3. The buyer is also deemed to have accepted the goods when after the lapse of a reasonable time he retains them the goods without intimating to the seller that he has rejected them (s35(4)).
4. The problem is balancing the need for finality in commercial transactions against consumer rights. Prior to 1995 this balance was tipped against the consumer (*Bernstein v Pamson Motors (Golders Green) Ltd* (1987)).

5. The Sale of Goods (Amendment) Act 1994 amended the SGA 1979 to give greater protection to consumers regarding acceptance of goods.

6. Under s35(6) the buyer is not deemed to have accepted the goods merely because:
   - he asks for, or agrees to, their repair by or under an arrangement with the seller; or
   - the goods are delivered to another under a sub-sale or other disposition.

7. This was applied in *Clegg v Andersson* (2003) where the claimant was held to have rejected the goods (a yacht) some six months after the contract. There were special circumstances as he had requested information from the defendant which had been slow to arrive and the claimant rejected the yacht within three weeks of getting the information.

8. S35(2) now states that where goods are delivered to the buyer and he has not previously examined them, he is not deemed to have accepted them until he has had a reasonable opportunity of examining them for the purpose of:
   - ascertaining whether they are in conformity with the contract; and
   - in the case of a sale by sample, comparing the bulk with the sample.

9. Consumers are further protected as, under s35(3), they cannot lose their rights by agreement or waiver. This covers situations where a buyer signs for goods without being able to examine them.

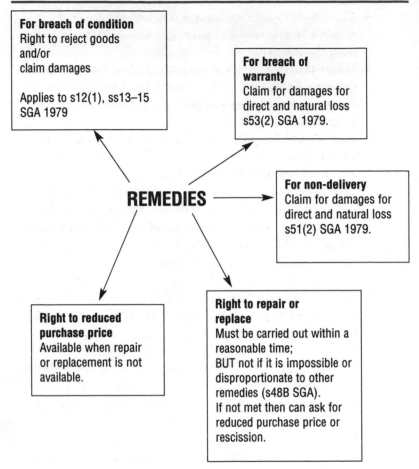

For breach of condition
Right to reject goods
and/or
claim damages

Applies to s12(1), ss13–15
SGA 1979

For breach of warranty
Claim for damages for direct and natural loss s53(2) SGA 1979.

REMEDIES

For non-delivery
Claim for damages for direct and natural loss s51(2) SGA 1979.

Right to reduced purchase price
Available when repair or replacement is not available.

Right to repair or replace
Must be carried out within a reasonable time;
BUT not if it is impossible or disproportionate to other remedies (s48B SGA).
If not met then can ask for reduced purchase price or rescission.

3.8 REMEDIES

1. A consumer buyer has the right to reject the goods where there is a breach of s12(1) or ss13–15.
2. In addition, the buyer may claim damages for personal injuries caused by the breach (*Godley v Perry* (1960)).
3. The buyer may also claim for loss arising naturally from the breach under the normal rules of contract. (*Hadley v Baxendale* (1854); *Koufos v Czarnikow (The Heron II)* (1969).)

4. There is also a right to damages for non-delivery of goods which is 'the estimated loss directly and naturally resulting ... from the seller's breach of contract' (s51(2)).

5. Where there is a breach of warranty the buyer can claim damages. Again the measure of damages is the estimated loss directly and naturally resulting ... from the seller's breach of contract' (s53(2)).

6. The Sale and Supply of Goods to Consumers Regulations 2002 inserted new sections into the SGA 1979, giving additional remedies to consumers.

7. The first of these is the right to repair or replacement of the goods (s48B). The seller must do this within a reasonable time of request without causing significant inconvenience to the buyer. The right is not available if:
   (a) the remedy is impossible;
   (b) it is disproportionate in comparison to other remedies.

8. Where repair or replacement is not available, the buyer has a right to require the seller to reduce the purchase price or to rescind the contract (s48C(2)(a)).

9. Where a request of repair or replacement has not been met within a reasonable time, the buyer has a right to require the seller to reduce the purchase price or to rescind the contract (s48C(2)(b)).

CHAPTER 4

UNSOLICITED GOODS

Definition
Goods sent to a person
without their requesting
them.

UNSOLICITED GOODS

Civil law
Where the goods are not
for business and there is
no agreement to acquire
or return the goods, then:
- the recipient may use,
  deal with or dispose of
  the goods as if they
  were an absolute gift;
- the sender's rights are
  extinguished
(reg 24 Consumer
Protection (Distance
Selling) Regulations
2000).

Criminal law
Offences:
- to make a demand for
  payment;
- to assert a right to
  payment;
- to threaten to bring legal
  proceedings;
- to place or threaten to
  place names on
  defaulters list;
- to invoke any other
  collection procedure
(Unsolicited Goods and
Services Act 1971;
2000 Regulations).

4.1 BACKGROUND

1. Unsolicited goods are those which are sent to a person
   without their requesting them.
2. This caused problems for consumers where such a delivery
   was followed by aggressive sales tactics, eg sending an invoice
   for the price.

3. This problem was originally overcome by the Unsolicited Goods and Services Act 1971 which gave protection in both civil law and criminal law.

4.2 CIVIL LAW

1. The civil law (previously covered by the Unsolicited Goods and Services Act 1971) is now covered by the Consumer Protection (Distance Selling) Regulations 2000.
2. Regulation 24 applies where:
   - unsolicited goods are sent to a person (the recipient) with a view to his acquiring them; and
   - the recipient has no reasonable cause to believe that they were sent with a view to their being acquired for the purpose of business; and
   - the recipient has not agreed to acquire the goods or to return them.
3. Where these conditions are fulfilled, regulation 24(2) provides that, as between the recipient and the sender, the recipient may use, deal with or dispose of the goods as if they were an absolute gift.
4. The Regulations also provide that the rights of the sender to the goods are extinguished (reg 24(3)).
5. These regulations are stricter than the previous law, where recipients could not dispose of the goods right away but had to retain them for a certain time first.

4.3 CRIMINAL LAW

1. S2 of the Unsolicited Goods and Services Act 1971 and regulations 24(4) and 24(5) of the 2000 Regulations make it an offence for a trader to make a demand for payment for what he knows are unsolicited goods and for which he has no reasonable cause to believe that there is a right to payment.
2. It is also an offence to:
   - assert a right to payment; or

- threaten to bring legal proceedings in respect of the goods; or
- place or threaten to place the name of any person on a defaulter list; or
- invoke or threaten to invoke any other collection procedure.

CHAPTER 5

DISTANCE SELLING

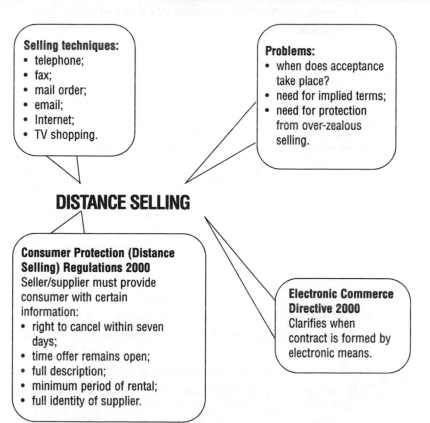

Selling techniques:
- telephone;
- fax;
- mail order;
- email;
- Internet;
- TV shopping.

Problems:
- when does acceptance take place?
- need for implied terms;
- need for protection from over-zealous selling.

DISTANCE SELLING

Consumer Protection (Distance Selling) Regulations 2000
Seller/supplier must provide consumer with certain information:
- right to cancel within seven days;
- time offer remains open;
- full description;
- minimum period of rental;
- full identity of supplier.

Electronic Commerce Directive 2000
Clarifies when contract is formed by electronic means.

5.1 MODERN SELLING TECHNIQUES

1. In the latter half of the twentieth century, numerous modern technological developments affected the means of contracting.
2. Telegraph, telegram and the fax all threw up problems in determining when a contract was formed – see, eg (*Entores v Miles Far East Corporation* (1955)).

3. In *Brinkibon Ltd v Stahag Stahl* (1983) Lord Wilberforce recognised the difficulties inherent in modern methods of communication. He suggested that 'No universal rule can cover all such cases; they must be resolved by reference to the intention of the parties, by sound business practice and in some cases by a judgment where the risk should lie.'

4. Communication by e-mail in forming contracts and use of the Internet for 'e-shopping' are more recent methods of contracting, with the same problems, and there was an obvious need for regulation to protect consumers.

5.2 THE CONSUMER PROTECTION (DISTANCE SELLING) REGULATIONS 2000

1. The Regulations were introduced to give effect to the EU Distance Selling Directive 97/7.

2. Inevitably, because of the potentially international scope of these new means of contracting, one of the key purposes of the Directive was the harmonisation of rules within the member states of the European Union.

3. The Regulations introduced by statutory instrument were a means of ensuring both clarity and protection of consumers in a whole range of modern methods of trading.

4. The Regulations apply to contracts for the sale of goods and for the provisions of services made by a variety of modern methods, eg:
   - telephone;
   - fax;
   - Internet shopping;
   - mail order;
   - e-mail;
   - television shopping.

5. The Regulations do not apply in certain identified contracts:
   - transfers of land (although electronic conveyancing is on the way);

- building contracts;
- financial services;
- purchases from vending machines;
- auctions.

6. For the protection of the consumer by regulation 7, the seller/supplier is now bound to provide the purchaser with certain minimum information before the contract can be considered validly formed.

7. These include:
   - the right to cancel the contract within seven days;
   - the length of time for which the offer will remain open;
   - full description of all matters relating to the contract;
   - the price;
   - the appropriate arrangements for payment and delivery and performance (and for how long all of these remain open);
   - the minimum period of the contract if it relates to something like mobile phone rental;
   - the full identity of the supplier.

8. Implied terms stemming from the Regulations also offer the consumer other significant protections.

9. By regulation 8 the seller must give written confirmation of all details relating to the contract or by e-mail or fax.

10. Inevitably, if these rules are not complied with then the contract is not formed and is not enforceable against the prospective buyer.

11. The Regulations also operate by including a number of implied terms in contracts entered into by such means, which the seller will be expected to comply with in order for that transaction to be binding.

12. Significantly, regulation 10 also offers the protection that the consumer must be informed of his/her right to cancel the contract within seven days. Regulation 7(4) also requires that in telephone communications the seller must make his/her identity and the purpose of the call known to the consumer at the start of the phone call.

13. There are more complex rules regarding cancellation in regulation 11 for sale of goods contracts and regulation 12 in the case of supply of goods and services contracts.
14. Regulation 14 requires that where the consumer does cancel the contract, his/her money must be returned within a maximum of 30 days from the date of cancellation.
15. The Regulations are also enforced by Trading Standards departments through the means of criminal sanctions and are under the general control of the Director General of Fair Trading.

5.3 THE ELECTRONIC COMMERCE DIRECTIVE 2000/31

1. This Directive regulates the formation of contracts by electronic means.
2. Article 11 says that 'where *[a purchaser]* in accepting *[a seller's]* offer is required to give his consent through technological means, such as clicking on an icon, the contract is concluded when the recipient of the service has received from the service provider, electronically, an acknowledgement of receipt of the recipient's acceptance'.
3. So this would appear to clear up some of the problems formerly encountered in determining when such agreements are actually complete and a contract is formed.

CHAPTER 6

SUPPLY OF GOODS AND SERVICES

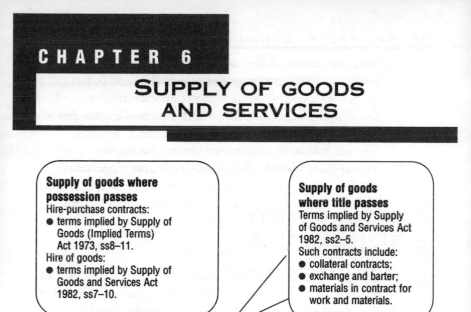

Supply of goods where possession passes
Hire-purchase contracts:
● terms implied by Supply of Goods (Implied Terms) Act 1973, ss8–11.
Hire of goods:
● terms implied by Supply of Goods and Services Act 1982, ss7–10.

Supply of goods where title passes
Terms implied by Supply of Goods and Services Act 1982, ss2–5.
Such contracts include:
● collateral contracts;
● exchange and barter;
● materials in contract for work and materials.

IMPLIED TERMS IN CONTRACTS FOR THE SUPPLY OF GOODS AND SERVICES

Supply of services
Terms implied by Supply of Goods and Services Act 1982, ss13–15:
● reasonable skill and care;
● carried out within a reasonable time;
● carried out for a reasonable consideration.

6.1 BACKGROUND

1. Protection for consumers in sale of goods contracts has existed since 1893 (the original Sale of Goods Act). However, this did not provide consumer protection in other contracts involving the supply of goods.

2. Statutory protection for consumers in other contracts has been provided by the Supply of Goods (Implied Terms) Act 1973, which covers hire-purchase contracts, and the Supply of Goods and Services Act 1982 which covers other transfers of goods and hire of goods.

3. The first statutory consumer protection for the supply of services came with the Supply of Goods and Services Act 1982.

6.2 CONTRACTS OF HIRE-PURCHASE

1. In a contract of hire-purchase, the consumer agrees to hire the goods with an option to purchase them (usually at the end of the period of hire when the hirer has completed the payments).

2. The Supply of Goods (Implied Terms) Act 1973, s8 implies a condition that the owner will have the right to sell when the property is to pass to the hirer, ie usually at the end of the period of hire.

3. Ss9–11 of the same Act imply terms about:
   ● description;
   ● quality and fitness;
   ● corresponding with samples.

4. These terms in respect of these three matters are identical with those in ss13–15 of the Sale of Goods Act 1979 (see Chapter 3).

5. Under the Unfair Contracts Terms Act 1977, s8 cannot be excluded from any contract and ss9–11 cannot be excluded from a consumer contract.

6.3 OTHER CONTRACTS FOR THE SUPPLY OF GOODS

1. The Supply of Goods and Services Act 1982 covers contracts where there is a transfer of property in goods other than contracts for sale of goods or contracts of hire-purchase.

2. These include:

- collateral contracts, such as free gifts (*Esso Petroleum Co. v Commissioners of Custom and Excise* (1976)) which was not covered by the Sale of Goods Act;
- exchange and barter contracts, eg where goods are exchanged for tokens or where they are exchanged for other goods;
- materials in contracts for work and materials, ie contracts which are primarily for a service but which also involve a transfer of goods, eg a car service where new brake linings are fitted or repairs to a tap by a plumber in which a new washer is fitted.

3. For all these contracts, the Supply of Goods and Services Act 1982, ss2–5 imply the same terms as in the Sale of Goods Act 1979, ss12–15 regarding:

- title;
- description;
- quality and fitness;
- correspondence with sample.

4. The effect of the Supply of Goods and Services Act 1982 is that in all situations where goods are transferred to a consumer, that consumer has exactly the same rights as consumers in sale of goods contracts.

5. The Unfair Contracts Terms Act 1977 provides that these implied terms cannot be excluded from a consumer contract.

6.3.1 Contracts for the hire of goods

1. Under a contract for hire there is no intention of transferring ownership of the goods (s6 of the Supply of Goods and Services Act 1982).

2. As no title passes in a contract for hire, s7 of that Act implies a term that the bailor has the right to transfer possession of the goods.

3. Ss8–10 imply the same terms in respect of description, quality and fitness, and correspondence to sample as in sale of goods contracts (see Chapter 3).

As seen from the above, the same terms regarding description, quality and fitness, and correspondence to sample are implied into all contracts for sale or supply of goods. However, the specific statute relied on varies according to the type of contract. This is shown in the table below.

Implied term	Type of contract	Relevant act /section
Title	Sale of goods	s12 Sale of Goods Act 1979
	Hire-purchase	s8 Supply of Goods (Implied Terms) Act 1977
	Hire of goods (right to transfer possession)	s7 Supply of Goods and Services Act 1982
	Other contracts for the supply of goods	s2 Supply of Goods and Services Act 1982
Description Quality and fitness Corresponding to sample	Sale of goods	ss13–15 Sale of Goods Act 1979
	Hire-purchase	ss9–11 Supply of Goods (Implied Terms) Act 1977
	Hire of goods (right to transfer possession)	ss8–10 Supply of Goods and Services Act 1982
	Other contracts for the supply of goods	ss3–5 Supply of Goods and Services Act 1982

6.4 CONTRACTS FOR SERVICES

1. A contract for services is one where the supplier agrees to carry out a service. This covers a wide range of contracts, eg repair, decorating, cleaning, carriage of goods or passengers, provision of accommodation, haircuts, insurance, accountancy, dental care, and so on.

2. A report in 1981, *Service Please* (Lantin and Woodroffe) highlighted that consumers of services were particularly dissatisfied with:
   - the quality of work;
   - the time it took to do it; and
   - the cost.

3. This report led to the passing of the Supply of Goods and Services Act 1982.

4. Some contracts of service are excluded from the provisions of s13 of the Supply of Goods and Services Act 1982. These are:
   - contracts of employment and apprenticeships (s12(2));
   - the services of an advocate in court or other tribunal or carrying out preliminary work directly affecting the conduct of the hearing;
   - the services rendered to a company by a director of the company;
   - the service provided by arbitrators.

5. The Supply of Goods and Services Act 1982 implies terms in respect of:
   - reasonable care and skill (s13);
   - reasonable time for performance (s14);
   - reasonable consideration (s15).

6. The terms implied into contracts for services are less onerous than those implied into contracts in respect of goods.

6.4.1 Reasonable care and skill

1. S13 implies a term that the supplier will carry out the contract with reasonable care and skill.

2. This section only applies where the supplier is acting in the course of business.

3. The use of the word 'reasonable' means that the standard of care is the same as in the tort of negligence.

4. This term cannot be excluded where the person to whom the service is provided is dealing as a consumer or where the supply was on the basis of a standard form contract (s3 Unfair Contract Terms Act 1977).

5. The statute uses the word 'term', so it may be either a condition or a warranty, depending on the circumstances. To decide which it is, the *Hong Kong* test for innominate terms will apply (*Hong Kong Fir Shipping Co. Ltd v Kawasaki Kisen Kaisha Ltd* (1962)).

6. This means that where there is a breach, the consumer may be able to discharge the contract or may have only the right to damages.

6.4.2 Reasonable time for performance

1. S14 provides an implied term that the supplier will carry out the service within a reasonable time.
2. This section only applies where the supplier is acting in the course of business.
3. It only applies where the time for the service to be carried out is not fixed by the contract, left to be determined by the parties or determined by the course of dealing between the parties.
4. What is a 'reasonable time' is a question of fact (s14(2)). This means that it will vary depending on the type of service being supplied and other factors, such as the availability of materials.
5. The length of time that a competent repairer etc would take can be considered (*Charnock v Liverpool Corporation* (1968)).

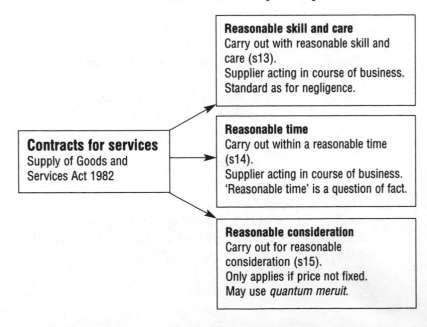

Contracts for services
Supply of Goods and Services Act 1982

Reasonable skill and care
Carry out with reasonable skill and care (s13).
Supplier acting in course of business.
Standard as for negligence.

Reasonable time
Carry out within a reasonable time (s14).
Supplier acting in course of business.
'Reasonable time' is a question of fact.

Reasonable consideration
Carry out for reasonable consideration (s15).
Only applies if price not fixed.
May use *quantum meruit*.

6.4.3 Consideration for the service

1. S15 implies a term that the party contracting with the supplier will pay a reasonable charge.
2. This only applies where the consideration for the service is:
   - not determined by the contract;
   - left to be determined in a manner agreed by the contract or the parties; or
   - determined by the course of dealing between the parties.
3. However, the common law may apply to vary an excessive charge (*Interfoto Picture Library Ltd v Stiletto Visual Programmes Ltd* (1988)).
4. What is reasonable is a question of fact for each case. Common law rules on *quantum meruit* may be applied where work has been partially completed (*Way v Latilla* (1937)).

CHAPTER 7

PROTECTION UNDER THE LAW OF TORT

Common law liability:
- Traditionally, actions were only available in contract law.
- Some limited tort liability for 'goods capable of doing mischief' (*Dixon v Bell*).
- General duty rejected because of lack of privity of contract (*Winterburn v Wright*).
- General duty established for known defects causing danger (*Heaven v Pender*).
- Modern liability comes from case of *Donoghue v Stevenson* – manufacturer liable to ultimate consumer for defects when intends goods to reach ultimate consumer with no intermediate examination.

PRODUCT LIABILITY IN TORT

Goods, defendants, claimants

Goods

Applied first to food (*Donoghue v Stevenson*), then added all manufactured goods (*Grant v Australian Knitting Mills*) and now any product in domestic use (*St Albans City and District Council v International Computers Ltd*).

Defendants

'Manufacturers' now includes wholesalers, retailers, assemblers, even repairers (*Haseldine v Daw*).

Claimants

Claimants are 'ultimate consumers', eg now includes suppliers injured by the goods (*Barnett v H and J Packer*) and even bystanders (*Stennet v Hancock*).

Elements of liability
- Usual elements of negligence.
- Duty is distributing defective goods where there will be no intermediate inspection.
- Breach of duty is failing to rectify known defects (*Grant v Australian Knitting Mills*).
- There must be no other known cause (*Evans v Triplex Safety Glass*) or no negligent inspection that would reveal defect (*Griffiths v Arch Engineering*).
- Can recover for all damage caused by defects (*Aswan Engineering v Lupdine*).
- But not pure loss of value (*Muirhead v Industrial Tank*).

7.1 INTRODUCTION

1. Product liability is only one aspect of consumer protection.
2. So its origins are in contract law:
   - although *caveat emptor*, traditionally applied;
   - effective consumer protection began with the Sale of Goods Act 1893, which implied into contracts terms as to quality of the goods.
3. Otherwise there were only limited opportunities to sue in tort in respect of dangerous goods.
4. Suing in contract had obvious shortcomings:
   - remedies were only available to the **parties** to the contract
   - damages limited to loss of bargain, reliance loss and restitution.
5. So a doctrine of tortious liability for defective goods developed.

7.2 THE DEVELOPMENT OF COMMON-LAW LIABILITY FOR DEFECTIVE PRODUCTS IN TORT

1. The earliest liability for defective goods was *Dixon v Bell* (1816) – liability for entrusting a gun to a young servant who was injured because the goods were 'capable of doing mischief'.
2. Originally, general claims for defective or dangerous goods were rejected because of lack of privity of contract (*Langridge v Levy* (1837); (*Winterbottom v Wright* (1842)).
3. Possibility of a general claim in tort independent of contractual relationship came in *Heaven v Pender* (1883) – but only for known defects for which no warning was given by the supplier.
4. The first real acceptance of general tortious liability for defective goods came in *Donoghue v Stevenson* (1932) where

Lord Atkin exploded the 'privity myth' – and distinguished from the other cases where he felt that the relationship was too distant for a duty to be imposed.

7.3 LIABILITY FOR DEFECTIVE PRODUCTS UNDER *DONOGHUE v STEVENSON*

7.3.1 The basis of liability

1. Tort liability for defective products under negligence derives from Lord Atkin's 'narrow *ratio*' in *Donoghue v Stevenson*.
2. Lord Atkin identified that 'a manufacturer of products which he sells in such form as to show that he intends them to reach the ultimate consumer in the form in which they left him with no reasonable possibility of intermediate examination, and with the knowledge that the absence of reasonable care in the preparation or putting up of the products will result in an injury to the consumer's life or property, owes a duty to the consumer to take reasonable care'.
3. Development of the tort has been through use of Lord Atkin's 'broad rule' – the 'neighbour principle'.

7.3.2 The scope of liability

1. The tort is not concerned with the quality of goods – but the damage that they cause:
   * so damage must be physical and not purely economic (see *Murphy v Brentwood DC* (1990));
   * and claims over quality should be made in contract law.
2. At first the tort applied only to foodstuffs (*Donoghue v Stevenson*).
3. But has been extended to include anything manufactured (*Grant v Australian Knitting Mills* (1936) – liability when

underpants still containing a chemical caused dermatitis in the wearer).

4. And now applies to all products in domestic use, eg:
   - motor cars (*Herschtal v Stewart and Arden Ltd* (1940));
   - houses, including fixtures and fittings (*Batty v Metropolitan Property Realisations Ltd* (1978));
   - lifts (*Haseldine v Daw Ltd* (1941));
   - and more recently even computer software (*St Albans City and District Council v International Computers Ltd* (1996)).

7.3.3 Potential defendants

1. Potential defendants were originally 'manufacturers'.
2. This was a narrow concept but it has been expanded.
3. It now includes, eg:
   - wholesalers (*Watson v Buckley, Osborne Garrett & Co. Ltd* (1940): failing to test hair dye);
   - retailers (*Kubach v Hollands* (1937): failing to follow manufacturer's instructions on testing before labelling);
   - suppliers of goods (where the duty extends beyond mere distribution: *Herschtal v Stewart and Arden Ltd* (1940));
   - repairers (*Haseldine v Daw Ltd* (1941));
   - assemblers (if under a duty to inspect the goods) (*Malfroot v Noxal Ltd* (1935)).

7.3.4 Potential claimants

1. Potential claimants were originally any 'ultimate consumers'.
2. Again, the concept is now broadened so that it includes anyone the 'manufacturer' should see as being affected by his actions.
3. This can include:
   - suppliers injured by the goods (*Barnett v H and J Packer & Co.* (1940): metal protruding from the goods injuring a retailer);

- mere bystanders (*Stennet v Hancock* (1939): pedestrian injured by reassembled component falling off lorry);
- and certainly includes people receiving goods as presents or even those borrowing goods.

7.3.5 Intermediate examinations

1. The original rule concerned situations where the manufacturer supplied the goods in a form where there was no possibility of intermediate examination, eg by the retailer.
2. And the test is therefore stricter than for other forms of negligence (*Clay v A J Crump & Sons Ltd* (1964)).

7.3.6 The elements of a claim for negligence for defective products

1. Bringing an action is the same as for negligence – the claimant must show:
   - duty of care owed by manufacturer to 'ultimate consumer';
   - breach of the duty by the defendant; and
   - a causal link with the damage suffered.
2. Breach is eg a failure in the production process (*Grant v Australian Knitting Mills* (1936)):
   - and can include failing to do anything about a known fault (*Walton v British Leyland* (1978): cars were not recalled once the defect was detected so there was liability);
   - but manufacturer can avoid liability if it can show that the cause of the defect did not arise through want of care on its part (*Daniels and Daniels v R White & Sons Ltd and Tarbard* (1938));
   - detailed knowledge of manufacturing processes is beyond the capability of most consumers;
   - this places a very heavy burden of proof on the claimant and so the doctrine *res ipsa loquitur* may be appropriate.

3. Causation will also be proved only if:
   - there is no other cause for defects in the product – so the chain of distribution can be a problem for the claimant (*Evans v Triplex Safety Glass* (1936): no liability on manufacturer for a shattered windscreen because fault could have developed anywhere in the chain of production and distribution);
   - there is no negligent inspection of the goods by claimant which should have revealed the defect (*Griffiths v Arch Engineering Co* (1968): but to expect a purchaser to wash clothes before wearing them is not reasonable);
   - causation can be problematic in the case of certain types of goods, eg pharmaceuticals (*Loveday v Renton* (1990)).
4. Can recover for damage caused by defects in goods (*Aswan Engineering Establishment Co. v Lupdine Ltd* (1987)).
5. But cannot recover for a pure loss of value in the goods themselves (*Muirhead v Industrial Tank Specialities Ltd* (1985): pumps for storing live lobsters were defective but claimants could not recover from loss of profit for sale of lobsters they had bought but had been unable to store).
6. Clearly, the two most important problems of the tort are:
   - the difficulty of proving causation; and
   - the difficulty of establishing fault.

The Thalidomide cases (settled out of court) are evidence of both these points.

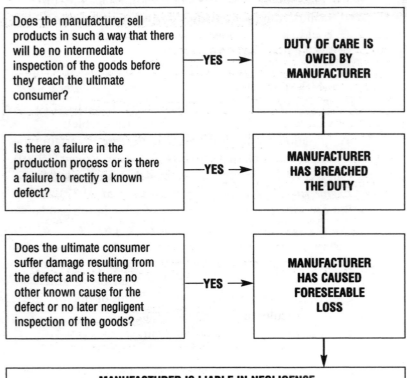

CONTROL OF EXEMPTION CLAUSES AND UNFAIR TERMS

Incorporation of the clause into the contract:
- A party is bound by a written agreement (s)he has signed (*L'Estrange v Graucob*).
- A party is only bound by a clause that (s)he knew of when the contract was formed (*Olley v Marlborough Court Hotel*).
- Knowledge can be implied from past dealings (*Spurling v Bradshaw*).
- But actual knowledge is required when past dealings are inconsistent (*McCutcheon v MacBrayne*).
- The party wanting to rely on the clause must properly draw it to the attention of the other party (*Parker v S.E. Railway Co.*).
- A ticket with the clause on the reverse is insufficient (*Chappleton v Barry UDC*).
- Non-specific references to other documents are also insufficient notice (*Dillon v Baltic Shipping Co. (The Mikhail Lermontov)*).
- And the clause may need to be dramatically brought to the other party's attention (*Thornton v Shoe Lane Parking*).
- The rule may apply to other onerous terms, not just exclusion clauses (*Interfoto Picture Library v Stiletto Visual Programmes Ltd*).

JUDICIAL CONTROL OF EXCLUSION CLAUSES

Construction of the contract:
- Even an incorporated clause can fail on construction of the contract as a whole.
- *Contra preferentem* can apply (*Andrews Bros v Singer*).
- Any ambiguity works against the party including the clause (*Hollier v Rambler Motors*).
- Can apply to other types of terms (*Vaswani v Italian Motor Cars Ltd*).
- Where breach is serious, standard-form terms can be strictly construed (*Computer & System Engineering v John Lelliott Ltd*).
- Originally a 'fundamental breach' was treated as if the whole contract was breached and exclusion clauses could not be relied on (*Karsales v Wallis*).
  - Judges dislike the doctrine (*The Suisse Atlantique case*).
  - Allowed exclusions freely negotiated if bargaining strength is equal (*Photo Productions v Securicor Transport*).
  - Providing the clause is clear and unambiguous (*Ailsa Craig Fishing v Malvern Fishing*).
  - Though a clause may be measured against statutory concepts such as reasonableness (*George Mitchell v Finney Lock Seeds*).

Other limitations:
- Oral misrepresentations about the clause can invalidate it (*Curtiss v Chemical Cleaning Co.*).
- Oral promises can override written terms (*J Evans & Son (Portsmouth) Ltd v Andrea Merzario Ltd*).
- Collateral promises can override exclusion clauses (*Webster v Higgin*).
- Third parties cannot rely on protection of an exclusion clause (*Scruttons v Midland Silicones Ltd* – but see *New Zealand Shipping v Satterthwaite (The Eurymedon)*).

8.1 JUDICIAL CONTROL OF EXEMPTION CLAUSES

8.1.1 Definition and scope of exemption clauses

1. An exclusion clause (exemption clause) is a term in a contract aiming to exclude the liability of the party inserting it from liability for his/her contractual breaches or even for torts.
2. A limitation clause merely restricts the extent of the liability.
3. Both types of clause are harsh on a party who is of weaker bargaining strength (including consumers).
4. Previously, such clauses would be binding because of the maxim *caveat emptor* (let the buyer beware) – the other party had to try to negotiate a contract without the clause in it. Even the Sale of Goods Act 1893 allowed for such clauses.
5. The late twentieth century saw moves towards consumer protection – by the courts, statute and EU law all regulating such clauses.
6. There are three elements to judicial recognition of exclusion clauses:
   - the clause must be actually incorporated into the contract – to show that it is part of the contract and can be relied upon;
   - construction of the contract must show that the clause actually protects the party inserting it for the damage in question – and thus no advantage is gained from doubt or ambiguity;
   - other tests may be applied if appropriate.

8.1.2 Incorporation of exclusion clauses

1. Rules on incorporation of exclusion clauses are interchangeable with those for incorporation of terms generally.
2. Parties are generally bound by the terms of any agreement they have signed (*L'Estrange v Graucob* (1934)).

3. Parties are only bound by an exclusion clause of which they had express knowledge at the time the contract was formed (*Olley v Marlborough Court Hotel* (1949)). The exclusion of liability for articles stolen in a hotel was in the room and so was inoperative.

- Parties who have previously contracted on the same terms are deemed to have express knowledge of the clause and so are bound by it (*Spurling v Bradshaw* (1956)).

- But if past dealings were inconsistent only, actual knowledge of the clause is sufficient – it cannot be implied from past dealing (*McCutcheon v MacBrayne* (1964)). When a ferry sank with the claimant's car, a risk note was not given every time so the clause failed.

4. The party seeking to rely on the clause must have effectively brought it to the attention of the other party (*Parker v South Eastern Railway Co.* (1877)).

- Handing over a ticket with reference to the clause on the back is insufficient notice (*Chappleton v Barry UDC* (1952)).

- Unspecific references to the document containing a clause may also be insufficient to incorporate the clause (*Dillon v Baltic Shipping Co. Ltd (The Mikhail Lermontov)* (1991)).

- The duty to give notice can be strictly interpreted, particularly where the party subject to the clause has little opportunity to negotiate (*Thornton v Shoe Lane Parking* (1971)). A clause covering damage in a multi-storey car park failed because the car owner only took a ticket from a machine.

- Strict interpretation has also been applied to clauses that are merely onerous rather than excluding liability (*Interfoto Picture Library v Stiletto Visual Programmes Ltd* (1988)).

8.1.3 Construction of the contract

1. A successfully incorporated clause can still fail on construction of the contract as a whole.

2. The *contra preferentem* rule can apply if the wording of the clause is ambiguous (*Andrews Bros (Bournemouth) Ltd v Singer & Co.* (1934)).

- Ambiguous expression in the clause works against the party including it in the contract (*Hollier v Rambler Motors* (1972): a clause covering fire damage failed because it did not specify negligence).
- The rule is not limited only to construction of exclusion clauses (*Vaswani v Italian Motor Cars Ltd* (1996)).

3. Clauses in standard-form contracts may be strictly construed to invalidate them when the breach is serious (*Computer & System Engineering plc v John Lelliott Ltd* (1991)).

4. Originally, by the doctrine of 'fundamental breach' an exclusion clause might be inoperable because breach of a fundamental term was said to be breach of the whole contract (*Karsales (Harrow) v Wallis* (1956)).

- But this was destructive to freedom of contract, so it was not always applied (*Suisse Atlantique Société d'Armaments Maritimes SA v NV Rotterdamsche Kolen Centrale (The Suisse Atlantique case)* (1967)).
- Now courts will enforce exclusion clauses or limitation clauses that are freely and genuinely agreed when the contract was formed (*Photo Productions Ltd v Securicor Transport Ltd* (1980)) – if bargaining strength is equal, even with a dramatic breach, if the clause is clear and unambiguous then it can be relied upon (*Ailsa Craig Fishing Co. Ltd v Malvern Fishing Co. Ltd* (1983)).
- Since the Unfair Contract Terms Act 1977, courts might apply the test of reasonableness from the Act (*George Mitchell Ltd v Finney Lock Seeds Ltd* (1983)).

8.1.4 Other limitations on the use of exclusion clauses

1. Oral misrepresentations about the scope of an exclusion in a written contract may invalidate the clause, as it is the

misrepresentation that is relied on (*Curtiss v Chemical Cleaning Co. Ltd* (1951)). Compensation could be paid for chemical stains to a wedding dress. The assistant misrepresented the scope of the clause.

2. Terms in contracts (and so exclusion clauses) can be overridden by oral promises made before the contract was formed (*J Evans & Son (Portsmouth) Ltd v Andrea Merzario Ltd* (1976)).

3. As can collateral undertakings (*Webster v Higgin* (1948)).

4. Generally, contracts only bind the parties involved, so that an exclusion clause will not protect a third party from liability (*Scruttons v Midland Silicones Ltd* (1962)).

5. But there are some inroads into this principle (*New Zealand Shipping Co. Ltd v Satterthwaite & Co. Ltd (The Eurymedon)* (1975)).

Clauses void under UCTA:
Excluding liability for:
- death/personal injury;
- breaches of implied terms under ss12–15 Sale of Goods Act in consumer contracts;
- breaches of implied terms under ss3–5 in Sale and Supply of Goods Act 1982 in consumer contracts;
- any similar provisions in the Consumer Credit Act 1974.

Definition of 'consumer' in UCTA:
- One party contracts not in the course of a business, or not holding himself out as carrying out a business.
- The other party contracts in the course of a business.
- The goods are of a kind that are ordinarily supplied for private use or consumption.

STATUTORY CONTROL OF EXCLUSION CLAUSES

Contracts valid if reasonable under UCTA:
Excluding liability for:
- loss other than injury caused by negligence;
- in consumer or standard form contracts a different performance or no performance;
- in business dealings breaches of implied terms under ss13–15 Sale of Goods Act 1979;
- in business dealings breaches of the implied terms in the Supply of Goods and Services Act 1982;
- misrepresentation.

Unfair Terms in Consumer Contract Regulations 1999:
- apply to all consumer contracts;
- and any unfair term;
- provides range of examples of imbalances;
- and aims to remove any unfairness;
- there is a list of examples of unfair terms.

8.2 STATUTORY CONTROL OF EXCLUSION CLAUSES

1. Judge-made rules were traditionally used to control the use of unfair exclusions of liability in contracts.
2. Now the most effective control is found in statutory provisions, recently modified to comply with EC law and found in:
   - the Unfair Contract Terms Act 1977;
   - the Unfair Terms in Consumer Contracts Regulations 1999.
3. UCTA seriously curtails freedom of contract, and also applies to exclusions for torts as well as breaches of contract.
4. The 1999 Regulations replaced the Unfair Terms in Consumer Contracts Regulations 1994 which gave effect to EC Directive 93/13 on unfair terms:
   - the 1999 Regulations are closer to the Directive's wording;
   - the Directive's key objective was producing harmonious rules to replace widely divergent national ones;
   - the Regulations are narrower than UCTA as they only apply to consumers;
   - they are broader than UCTA as they apply to unfair terms generally, not just exclusions, and they impose stricter duties.

8.3 THE UNFAIR CONTRACT TERMS ACT 1977

8.3.1 Introduction

1. A most significant areas of consumer protection.
2. It does not, however, cover every type of exclusion or unfair term but can apply sometimes even where there is no contract.
3. It compensates for inequality in bargaining strength by:
   - making certain exclusion clauses automatically void;
   - distinguishing between consumer and inter-business contracts;

- introducing a test of reasonableness to be applied in the case of the latter and in the case of some standard forms.

4. The Act does not cover insurance contracts and certain others.

8.3.2 Exclusions rendered void by the Act

1. Certain types of exclusion clauses are invalid and cannot be relied upon by the person inserting them in the contract:

- by s2(1) there can be no valid exclusion for death or injury caused by the negligence of the party inserting the clause;
- by s5(1) in any consumer contract a clause excluding liability by reference to the terms of a guarantee fails in respect of defects caused by negligence in manufacture or distribution;
- by s6(1) exclusion for breach of s12 Sale of Goods Act 1979 (the implied condition as to title) is invalid;
- by s6(2) in any consumer contract any exclusion for breach of any of the implied conditions in the Sale of Goods Act 1979, s13 (description), s14(2) (satisfactory quality), s14(3) (fitness for the purpose) and s15 (sale by sample) is invalid;
- breaches of conditions in Schedule 4 to the Consumer Credit Act 1974 (similar to those in Sale of Goods Act) are also invalid;
- by s7(1) the same applies in respect of goods supplied under the Supply of Goods and Services Act 1982;
- by s7(2) in any consumer contract any exclusion for breach of the implied conditions in the Supply of Goods and Services Act 1982 ss3, 4 and 5 (similar to SGA terms).

2. Also, under the Consumer Protection Act 1987 there can be no valid exclusion for breaches of the general safety standards.

8.3.3 The distinction between consumer contracts and business contracts

1. The Act operates mainly for the protection of consumers.
2. 'Consumer contract' is defined in s12(1) as where:
   - one party contracts not in the course of a business, or not holding himself out as carrying out a business;
   - the other party does contract in the course of a business;
   - the goods are of a kind that are ordinarily supplied for private use or consumption.
3. A person claiming to be a 'business' to gain trade discount loses the protection of s12 and cannot claim to be a consumer.
4. By s14 business includes profession, central or local government.
5. By s12(3) it is for the party seeking to rely on the clause to disprove that it is a consumer contract.

8.3.4 Exclusions valid only if reasonable

The Act identifies a number of exclusions that will be valid only if they satisfy a test of reasonableness:
- by s2(2) an exclusion for loss other than death or injury caused by the negligence of the party inserting the clause;
- by s3 when one party deals as a consumer on the other party's standard forms exclusion for breach, a substantially different performance, or for no performance at all;
- by s7(3) exclusions for breaches of the implied conditions in the Supply of Goods and Services Act in ss3, 4, and 5
- by s8 exclusions for misrepresentations;
- by s4 indemnity clauses – compare *Thompson v T H Lohan (Plant Hire) Ltd & J W Hurdiss Ltd* with *Philips Products Ltd v Hyland* (1987).

8.3.5 The test of reasonableness

1. The Act does not define what is 'reasonable' but guidelines are set out in both s11 and in Schedule 2.

2. By s11(5) the burden of proving that the clause is reasonable is on the party wishing to rely on it (*Warren v Trueprint* (1986)).

3. By s11(1) one test is: was including the clause reasonable in the light of the knowledge of the parties on contracting?

4. By s11(2), for exclusions falling under either s6(3) or s7(3), the criteria in Schedule 2 should be considered:
   - was there comparable bargaining strength?
   - did the buyer receive any inducement or advantage?
   - were the goods manufactured or processed or adapted to meet the buyer's own specifications?
   - should the buyer have expected an exclusion clause based on trade custom?

5. By s11(4) in the case of limitation clauses the ability of the party relying on the clause to meet liability if necessary or to insure against it should also be considered.

6. Judges are willing to apply the criteria in Schedule 2 to exclusions and limitations generally (*George Mitchell v Finney Lock Seeds* (1983) and *Smith v Eric S Bush* (1990)).

8.4. THE UNFAIR TERMS IN CONSUMER CONTRACTS REGULATIONS 1999

8.4.1 The scope and purpose of the Regulations

1. Article 7(1) of Directive 93/13 requires that 'adequate and effective means exist to prevent the continued use of unfair terms in contracts concluded with consumers'.

2. The Regulations seek to achieve this by:
   - applying to unfair terms generally, not just exclusion clauses;
   - declaring invalid and non-binding any term found to be 'unfair' – although the rest of the contract can bind if it can continue without that term (reg. 8);

- providing a non-exhaustive list of examples of unfair terms in Schedule 2;
- providing the means for the Director General of Fair Trading to consider complaints (reg 10) – powers also exist for the 'qualifying bodies' to take action, eg the Directors General of electricity, gas and water, rail regulator, weights and measures authorities, and Consumers Association.

3. The Regulations apply only to 'consumer contracts':
- defined in regulation 4 as one made between a seller/supplier and a consumer;
- 'seller'/'supplier' is defined as 'any person who sells or supplies goods or services and who, in making a contract, is acting for purposes related to his business';
- 'consumer' is defined as 'any natural person ... acting for purposes ... outside his trade, business or profession'
- By regulation 5 a term is unfair that is not individually negotiated and is contrary to good faith – (ie in standard forms).

5. Regulation 6 identifies that the legislature is not concerned with the fairness of core terms such as price.

6. Regulation 7 is the *contra preferentem* rule in statutory form – the words of a term must be in 'plain intelligible language' and any ambiguity is construed in favour of the consumer.

8.4.2 Terms regarded as unfair under Schedule 2

The list is generally non-exhaustive but includes ones which:
(a) exclude liability for death or personal injury;
(b) inappropriately limit liability for inadequate performance or non-performance or which exclude a right of set-off;
(c) are binding on the consumer but optional to the seller;
(d) allow the seller to keep a deposit in the event of the consumer's cancellation but not the other way round;
(e) make a consumer in breach pay excessive compensation;
(f) allow the seller to terminate the contract but not the buyer;

(g) allow the seller to end the contract without reasonable notice – except where there are serious grounds for doing so;

(h) automatically extend a fixed-term contract when the deadline for the consumer to object is unreasonably early;

(i) irrevocably bind the consumer to terms he had no means to discover before the contract was made;

(j) allow the seller unilaterally to vary terms without a valid reason specified in the contract;

(k) allow the seller unilaterally to vary the character of the product or service supplied, without a valid reason;

(l) allow for price to be determined on delivery or for the seller to alter the price without letting the consumer cancel;

(m) give the seller the sole right to interpret the contract or to determine whether goods conform to the contract;

(n) limit the seller's obligations for his agent's promises

(o) oblige the consumer to fulfil all obligations but not the seller;

(p) give sellers the right, without agreement of the consumer, to transfer obligations which might then reduce the rights of the consumer under guarantees;

(q) exclude consumers' rights to take legal action or restrict evidence available to consumer or alter the burden of proof.

Consumer Protection Act 1987: – civil remedies

Gives effect to EC Directive 85/374 – Civil liability is imposed in s2(1)

Defendants:

- producers – including manufacturers, those abstracting the product or adding to it in an industrial process;
- importers, suppliers (eg retailers) and 'own-branders';
- anyone else in chain of manufacture or distribution.

Products covered:

- goods – anything growing or any ship, aircraft, vehicle;
- products – goods, parts of other products – but not buildings and nuclear power.

Defects covered:

- if safety is not such as persons are generally entitled to expect.

Types of damage covered:

- death and personal injury, loss or damage to property;
- but not damage under £275, business property or damage to defective property itself.

Limitation:

- within 3 years of learning of defect, damage, or identity of defendant;
- 10 years from date of knowledge for latent damage.

Possible defences:

- product complies with statute or EC Directive;
- defect did not exist when supplied;
- not supplied in course of business;
- D did not supply product;
- state of technological or scientific knowledge when goods supplied.

Criticisms of Act:

- does not apply to all products, defects or damage;
- strict limitation period;
- does not apply to disputes pre-1988;
- too many defences;
- more like negligence than strict liability.

9.1 GENERAL BACKGROUND TO THE ACT

1. The Consumer Protection Act 1987 (CPA) was the UK's response to the EC Directive on Product Liability (Directive 85/374).
2. The Directive required the harmonisation of law of member states on the issue of product liability.
3. The Act is both criminal and civil in content – civil liability is under Part 1; criminal regulation is under Part 2.
4. In its regulatory sense it has since been supplemented by the Product Safety Regulations 1994 (which again is a response to EC law in the 1992 Product Safety Directive).
5. It is at least arguable that the criminal sanctions under the Act provide ultimately a more effective control of defective products than common-law product liability.
6. The civil liability in the Act is identified in s2(1): 'where any damage is caused wholly or partly by a defect in a product, every person to whom subsection 2 applies shall be liable for the damage'.

9.2 CIVIL LIABILITY UNDER THE ACT

9.2.1 Those who can be sued under the Act

1. These are listed in s2(2) and include:
2. Producers – these are defined in s1(2) and include:
   - the manufacturer – who can be the manufacturer of the final product, but also manufacturers and assemblers of component parts, and also producers of raw materials;
   - a person who 'wins' or 'abstracts' products – eg someone who extracts minerals from the ground;
   - a person carrying out an industrial or other process which adds to the essential characteristic of the product – eg freezing vegetables.

3. Importers, suppliers and 'own-branders' are also defined in s2(2), and can be liable to the consumer in certain circumstances.
4. Importers – under s2(2)(c) will include anybody who in the course of a business imports a product from outside of the EU.
5. Suppliers – these are obviously retailers or equivalent persons:
   - ordinarily they will be liable only in contract law;
   - but under s2(3), where it is impossible to identify either a 'producer' or an importer, the supplier can be liable if the consumer has asked the supplier to identify the producer, within a reasonable time of the damage suffered, because it is impractical for the consumer to identify the producer, and the supplier has failed to identify or refuses to identify the producer (this means that businesses must keep records of their suppliers).
6. Own-branders – under s2(2)(b) would be eg supermarket chains:
   - while not producers, they effectively hold themselves out as producers by declaring a product to be their own brand;
   - they must indicate that someone else is producing the goods for them in order to avoid liability under the Act.
7. As a result of these definitions three important points can be made:
   - any person in the chain of manufacture and distribution is potentially liable;
   - liability is both joint and several – meaning that the consumer can sue the person with the most money or best insurance cover;
   - liability is strict – meaning that fault need not be proved.

9.2.2 Products covered by the Act

1. 'Product' is defined in s2(1):
   - 'any goods or electricity and (subject to subsection (3)) includes a product which is comprised in another product, whether by virtue of being a component part, raw material or otherwise'.

2. 'Goods' are defined in s45(1):
   - 'substances, growing crops, and things comprised in land by virtue of being attached to it and any ship, aircraft or vehicle'.
3. However, a number of things are specifically exempted from the scope of the Act:
   - buildings – because they are immovable – though building materials are included;
   - nuclear power;
   - agricultural produce which has not undergone an industrial process – the problem here is in defining what is an industrial process, eg would butchery be, in the light of the BSE and CJD problems?

9.2.3 Defects covered by the Act

1. 'Defect' is defined in s3(1):
   - '… if the safety of the product is not such as persons generally are entitled to expect, taking into account all the circumstances …'.
2. The courts can take into account a number of circumstances in defining safety:
   - the manner in which and purposes for which the product has been marketed, its get-up, the use of any mark in relation to the product and any instructions for, or warnings with respect to, doing or refraining from doing anything in relation to the product;
   - what might reasonably be expected to be done with or in relation to the product;
   - the time when the product was supplied by its producer to another.
3. Market can be important, eg toys and children:
   - but the use of warnings can be too;
   - in which case the way that a consumer uses products can relieve liability, eg fireworks not to be used indoors.
4. Defects in production or design, which render the product unsafe, will result in liability under the Act.

- However, the consumer may cause the damage by improper use, eg drying wet pets in microwaves.
5. Another important factor is time, because knowledge is always increasing:
   - so the question is: once knowledge has changed, should a producer recall all products sold, however long ago in the past?

9.2.4 Type of damage to which the Act applies

1. The Act covers death, personal injury and loss or damage to property caused by unsafe products.
2. Some limitations are placed on this:
   - no damages will be given in respect of small property damage under £275 – a consumer here would need to use basic contract law instead;
   - no damages will be awarded in respect of business property – so the property must have been intended for private use, occupation or consumption;
   - no damages are recoverable for loss or damage to the defective product itself.

9.2.5 Limitation

1. The claimant must begin proceedings within three years of becoming aware of the defect, the damage or the identity of the defendant or, If the damage is latent, the date of knowledge of the plaintiff provided that is within the 10-year period.
2. The court has discretion to override the three-year period in the case of personal injury.
3. In all cases there is an absolute cut-off point for claims of 10 years from the date that the product was supplied.

9.2.6 Defences

1. All defences are contained in s4 of the Act.

2. They include:

- that the product complies with statutory or EC obligations – and so the defect was an inevitable consequence of complying with that requirement, eg a chemical required by law to be in a product but which then turns out to be dangerous;
- the defect did not exist at the time it was supplied by the defendant – this might include, eg animal rights campaigners 'doctoring' baby food, but also the case where the defect arises in the subsequent product but not in the component;
- the product was not supplied in the course of a business;
- where the defendant can show that it was not him/her who actually supplied the product;
- where the state of technical or scientific knowledge at the relevant time was not such that the defendant could be expected to have discovered the defect – (*Roe v Minister of Health* (1954)) (precedes the Act but makes the same point) – this is highly controversial and out of step with the law in many other EC countries which follow the Directive's wording of when the product was put into circulation.

9.3 SOME CRITICISMS OF THE ACT

1. The Act was a step forward in a few ways:

- it has put producers on their guard, and requires knowledge of the need for appropriate checking and quality control;
- as a result, there is a greater likelihood of product recall;
- it also allows the consumer more chance of an action because (s)he has a greater range of potential defendants to choose from.

2. However, the Act has shortcomings too:
- it does not apply to all products, nor to all defects, nor to all damage;
- the limitation period is very strict;
- the Act in any case does not apply to products supplied before 1988;
- there are probably too many defences, making it difficult for a claimant to succeed;
- causation is still a requirement and the standard of care is very similar to negligence, making it too similar to negligence and not enough like the strict liability it is supposed to be.

CHAPTER 10

CRIMINAL LAW AS A MEANS OF CONSUMER PROTECTION

10.1 THE PURPOSE OF USING CRIMINAL LAW SANCTIONS FOR CONSUMER PROTECTION

1. Civil liability is concerned mainly with compensation for wrongs suffered as the result of defective products or services, usually either contractual breaches or tortious wrongs.
2. Criminal liability is used more as a deterrent and so works in the following ways:
   - to prevent traders from engaging in certain abuses that might harm consumers;
   - to make traders improve their business practices;
   - to set high but attainable standards.
3. Criminal law, then, is mainly regulatory in character.
4. So it is also statutory in nature.
5. It also operates by the creation of strict liability offences.
6. There are many examples of statutory provisions leading to criminal sanctions (some of which are explained in more detail in the following chapters).
7. These include:
   - the Consumer Protection Act 1987 (Part 2);
   - the Trade Descriptions Act 1968;
   - the Consumer Credit Act 1974.
8. And also:
   - the Food Safety Act 1990;
   - the Property Misdescriptions Act 1991.
9. Many other controls are introduced by statutory instrument.
10. The common feature is that the legislation is enforced by public bodies such as the Trading Standards Department.

10.2 STRICT LIABILITY

1. Strict liability means that, unlike other crimes, there is no requirement to prove *mens rea* (or criminal intent).

2. Usually there is a presumption of *mens rea* in crime – but this can be rebutted by the wording of the statute, eg the word 'knowingly' tends to indicate that there is no strict liability: *Pharmaceutical Society of Great Britain v Storkwain Ltd* (1986). Here, many offences created in the Medicines Act 1968 used the term 'knowingly' and therefore required *mens rea*. There was no such use of the word in s58 which prohibits selling certain substances without a prescription, so this was a strict liability offence.

3. Context and subject-matter can also be important in determining strict liability, eg Acts concerned with safety such, as the Consumer Protection Act 1987, are more likely to result in strict liability than Acts concerned with the consumer's economic protection, such as the Fair Trading Act 1973.

4. Courts will also take the view that if enforcement of the provision will lead to an improvement of business practices then this justifies strict liability (*Tesco Supermarkets Ltd v Nattrass* (1972)). Here, Lord Diplock stated: 'Consumer protection ... is achieved only if the occurrence of the prohibited acts or omissions is prevented. It is the deterrent effect of penal provisions which protects the consumer from the loss he would sustain if the offence were committed ... the most effective method of deterrence is to place upon the employer the responsibility of doing everything which lies within his power to prevent his employees from doing anything which will result in the commission of an offence. This is ... the justification for creating in the field of consumer protection ... offences of strict liability.'

5. Even so, most strict liability offences in consumer protection carry with them the defence of due diligence (where the trader can show that he has taken all reasonable precautions).

6. There are also many other common defences, including mistake, reliance on information supplied, and act or default of another party. Even accidental cause is accepted.

CHAPTER 11

THE CONSUMER PROTECTION ACT 1987 AND CRIMINAL LIABILITY

Consumer Protection Act 1987 – criminal sanctions:
Gives effect to EC Directive 85/374 – criminal liability is imposed by Part 2

General safety requirment:
- s10(1) offence to supply consumer with goods below general safety standard;
- s10(2) means not safe in light of all relevant circumstances.

Defences:
- s10(3) goods comply with safety standards;
- s10(4) goods are second hand or sold for export;
- s10 (4)(b) due diligence defence for retailers;
- but otherwise liability is strict.

Power to introduce regulations:
- Secretary of State has such power under s11;
- by s11(2) can cover composition, contents, design, packaging, need for introduction only on with approval, need for testing or warnings, even outright bans.

Notices:
- s13(1)(a): Secretary of State can serve a prohibition notice – prevents sales of goods;
- s13(1)(b): or make person supplying unsafe goods provide warnings at own expense;
- s14: any enforcement authority can issue suspension notice.

Enforcement:
- by Trading Standards Officers;
- can seize any goods for testing and inspect any premises;
- breach of any safety standard or any notice punishable by fines and imprisonment;
- by s16 goods can be forfeited and destroyed;
- liability is strict.

11.1 CRIMINAL SANCTIONS UNDER THE CONSUMER PROTECTION ACT 1987

11.1.1 General

1. Criminal liability for consumer is contained in Part 2 of the Act.
2. The Act in this respect is based on the idea that prevention is better than cure, eg there are 7,000 deaths in the home each year from accidents involving unsafe products.

3. The Act operates by imposing criminal sanctions on manufacturers, retailers and distributors of faulty and dangerous goods.

11.1.2 The general safety requirement

1. By s10(1) it is an offence to supply, offer or agree to supply, or to expose or possess for supply, any consumer goods which fail to comply with the general safety requirement.
2. By s10(2) goods will fail to comply with the requirement if they are not reasonably safe, having regard to all the circumstances including their presentation, instructions for use, published safety standards, and the existence of reasonable means for making them safer (including cost etc).

11.1.3 Defences

1. By s10(3) the fact that the goods comply with safety regulations or approved safety standards.
2. By s10(4) showing that the goods are second hand or are to be sold for export.
3. By s10(4)(b) retailers have a special defence if they can show that they neither knew of nor had any grounds to suspect that the goods did not comply with appropriate safety standards (the 'due diligence' defence).
4. However, subject to the due diligence defence, liability under s10 is generally strict.

11.1.4 The power to introduce regulations

1. By s11 the Secretary of State has the power to introduce any provisions considered appropriate for the purpose of ensuring safety.
2. S11(2) provides a non-exhaustive list of matters that can be covered in regulations:
   - composition of contents, design, construction, finish, packaging;

- the requirement that the goods should be 'approved';
- requirements in respect of testing and inspection;
- requirements for provision of warnings, instructions, and any other relevant information;
- the outright banning of specific products.

11.1.5 Notices

1. By s13(1)(a), where the Secretary of State considers that specific goods are unsafe he may serve a 'prohibition notice' on a particular individual to prevent him from selling those goods.
2. By s13(1)(b), the Secretary of State may also require that a person who has supplied 'unsafe goods' should publish, in a prescribed manner and form, and at his own expense, a 'notice of warning'.
3. By s14, an officer of an enforcement authority may also serve a 'suspension notice' prohibiting further supply of the goods in circumstances where he believes that safety standards have been contravened.

11.1.6 Enforcement and sanctions

1. Enforcement is through local Trading Standards Departments.
2. Officers may make test purchases, enter premises to inspect goods, and seize goods for testing.
3. Contravention of any safety standards or of any notice is a summary offence and is punishable by both fines and periods of imprisonment.
4. By s16, unsafe goods can also be forfeited and even destroyed.
5. Again, liability is generally strict – though the defence of due diligence is possible.

11.2 THE PRODUCT SAFETY REGULATIONS 1994

1. The Regulations were enacted to comply with the Product Safety Directive of 1992.
   - The Directive was a necessary development in order to harmonise safety standards because of free movement of goods under Articles 28 and 29.
   - The Directive required: common safety standards; common enforcement procedures; the banning of unsafe goods; and the setting up of specific bodies to oversee product safety.
2. The Regulations supplement Part 2 of the Consumer Protection Act 1987.
3. The Regulations cover all goods intended for use by consumers or that are likely to be used by consumers:
   - this includes new goods but also second-hand or reconditioned goods;
   - so the Regulations are wider in scope than the Act;
   - and might include products that eventually reach a consumer in a different form, eg building or decorating materials.
4. Some products are specifically covered in EC law by other means and require specific implementation so are not within the scope of the Regulations, eg toys, which are covered by the Toy Safety Directive 88/378.
5. The Regulations impose duties on both 'producers' and 'distributors'.
6. 'Producers' include:
   - a manufacturer of a product;
   - a person reconditioning goods;
   - persons representing themselves as manufacturers by attaching their own labels to the goods;
   - importers of the goods into the EU;
   - others within the supply chain whose activities may possibly affect the safety of the goods, eg shopkeepers who remove safety labels or instructions.

7. Distributors include anybody in the chain of supply whose activities do not affect the safety of the product.

8. The basic duty on the producer is contained in regulation 7 – no producer shall place a product on the market unless the product is a safe product.

9. Breaches of the duty are considered in regulation 12.

10. Preparatory offences are covered in regulation 13 (this would include an agreement to place unsafe goods on the market).

11. Regulation 2(1) defines 'safe product' – one which presents no risk when under normal or reasonably foreseeable conditions of use (and this may of course include reasonably foreseeable conditions of misuse if safety is to be ensured).

12. Cost may be a relevant factor, eg air bags included in prestige cars but not on standard models (and therefore charged as an extra).

13. Various factors are used to assess whether or not the goods are safe:
    - the characteristics of the product, including composition, packaging, instructions for use, repair, maintenance etc;
    - the effect on other products in conjunction with which it may be used;
    - presentation, including labelling, instructions for use, instructions for disposal, and any other information supplied with the goods.

14. It may be sufficient under the Regulations that the goods comply with UK safety standards.

15. Producers are obliged to give all necessary information to consumers.

16. Distributors also owe a duty to act with 'due care' so that they may ensure compliance with the 'general safety requirement' – as a result, they have a supplementary duty to monitor goods for safety.

17. The Regulations, as with the Act, provide for criminal sanctions for breaches of the basic duty which include both fines and imprisonment.

CHAPTER 12

TRADE DESCRIPTIONS ACT 1968

False trade descriptions of goods
- applying a false trade description (s1(1)(a));
- supplying or offering to supply (s1(1)(b));
- by any person;
- in the course of trade or business;
- must be false to a material degree;
- includes descriptions in advertisements;
- does not include private transactions.

Misdescription of services
- making a statement which is known to be false (s14(1)(a));
- recklessly making a false statement (s14(1)(b));
- must be about services, accommodation or facilities;
- in the course of trade or business, including a profession;
- must be false to a material degree;
- does not include forecasts or promises about the future.

TRADE DESCRIPTIONS ACT 1968

Disclaimers
A statement making it clear that the representation cannot be relied on. To be effective, the disclaimer must:
- use very clear words;
- be as bold as the representation;
- be communicated before or at the same time as the trade description.

Defences:
S24(1) provides a general defence if the offence was committed:
- due to a mistake;
- by reliance on information provided by another or the act of another;
- an accident or some other cause beyond control

AND
the defendant took all reasonable precautions and exercised all due diligence.
S24(3) provides a special defence of innocent supply of goods.
S25 provides a defence of innocent publication of an advertisement.

12.1 FALSE TRADE DESCRIPTIONS IN RELATION TO GOODS

1. The Trade Descriptions Act 1968 (TDA) creates two offences of misdescription of goods. These are:
   - s1(1)(a): applying a false trade description to goods;
   - s1(1)(b): supplying or offering to supply goods to which a false trade description is applied.
2. Both of these are strict liability offences, though the Act does provide certain defences (see section 12.4).

12.1.1 'Goods'

'Goods' are defined in s39. It is a wide definition, including ships, aircraft, things attached to land and growing crops.

12.1.2 'Any person'

1. The offences can be committed by 'any person'. This includes a limited company.
2. Section 20 makes any director, manager, secretary or similar officer liable if the offence has been committed with their consent or connivance.
3. Normally the offence will be committed by the seller, but it is possible for a buyer to commit the offence (*Fletcher v Budgen* (1974)).
4. It is not necessary to be a party to the contract (*Fletcher v Sledmore* (1973)).

12.1.3 'In the course of trade or business'

1. The Act is not aimed at private sellers. It is restricted to commercial transactions (*Davies v Sumner* (1984)).
2. There must be some degree of regularity in dealing with the particular type of goods (*R & B Customs Brokers Co. Ltd v United Dominions Trust* (1988)).

3. A car dealer selling his own car is not acting in the course of business, even if that car has been used for purposes of his own business (*R v Shrewsbury Crown Court, ex parte Venables* (1994)).

4. However, a sale of a car by a car hire firm was in the course of business (*Havering London Borough v Stevenson* (1970)).

5. A private person doing something as a hobby is not acting in the course of business (*Blackmore v Bellamy* (1983)).

12.1.4 'Applies'

1. This is explained in s4 of the Act. It includes:
   (a) affixing or annexing to or marking the goods themselves or anything in, on or with which the goods are supplied;
   (b) placing the goods in, on, or with anything to which the trade description has been affixed or annexed or marked or incorporated;
   (c) using the trade description in any manner likely to be taken as referring to the goods.

2. In deciding whether a false trade description has been applied, an objective test is used, ie what a reasonable consumer might expect.

3. A description is applied where goods which were to be delivered are represented as being the same as display goods in the showroom (*Cavendish Woodhouse Ltd v Wright* (1985)).

4. A statement made after the sale is not applied to the goods for the purposes of the Act (*Hall v Wickens Motors Ltd* (1972)).

5. 'Any manner' has been held to include:
   - an active attempt to disguise a defect (*Cottee v Douglas Seaton (Used Cars) Ltd* (1972));
   - a description on an invoice or an order form;
   - a description in a trade journal (*Rees v Monday* (1974));
   - a misleading pictorial illustration.

6. Placing the goods in anything to which a description has been applied (s4(1)(b)) includes:
   - milk in bottles embossed with the name of another dairy (*Donnelly v Rowlands* (1970));

- where a petrol pump stated a different brand to that in the pump (*Roberts v Severn Petroleum and Trading Co. Ltd* (1981)).

12.1.5 'Trade description'

This is comprehensively defined in s2 of the Act which states that it includes the following matters:

(a) quantity, size or gauge: this includes such matters as height, length, capacity, weight, number; for this there does not have to be a written statement – it is sufficient if the packaging makes the product appear greater in quantity than it is (*R v A & F Pears Ltd* (1982));

(b) method of manufacture or production, eg hand-made, home-grown, free-range;

(c) composition;

(d) fitness for purpose, strength, performance, behaviour or accuracy, eg waterproof (*Sherratt v Gerald's* (1970)); or magnification capability (*Dixons Ltd v Barnett* (1989));

(e) any other physical characteristics;

(f) testing by any person and the results thereof;

(g) approval by any person or conformity with a type approved by any person;

(h) place or date of manufacture, production, processing or reconditioning; eg a 'Norfolk King Turkey' which had not been bred in Norfolk (*Beckett v Kingston Brothers (Butchers) Ltd* (1970));

(i) person who manufactured, produced, processed or reconditioned goods; but not if the goods are clearly labelled as copies of famous brand names (*Kent County Council v Price* (1993));

(j) other history, including previous ownership or use.

12.1.6 'False trade description'

1. To be false, a description must be false 'to a material degree' (s3(1) TDA 1968).

2. S3(2) extends this to cover descriptions which are not false but are misleading about any of the matters in s2 (see section 12.1.5) so that they would be false to a material degree.

3. This means that a statement which is literally true can be false under the Act if it is sufficiently misleading (*R v Inner London Justices, ex parte Wandsworth LBC* (1983)).

4. A description as to manufacturer is not false if it is clearly stated that the goods are a copy (*Kent County Council v Price* (1993)).

12.1.7 'Supplies or offers to supply'

1. S1(1)(b) of the TDA 1968 creates an offence of supplying or offering to supply goods to which a false trade description is applied.

2. Supply includes any form of distribution. This means that a contract of hire of goods is a form of supply even though the ownership of the goods does not pass to the consumer.

3. The supply must be of a commercial nature. The supply of goods by a private club to its members will not normally came within the Act (*John v Matthews* (1970)).

4. It can include returning goods to the owner where a false description of work done on the goods is made (*Formula One Autocentres Ltd v Birmingham CC* (1999)).

5. Offering to supply includes situations of 'exposing goods for supply or having goods in his possession for supply' (s6 TDA 1968).

6. This provision in s6 prevents any problems over the meaning of 'offer' in contract law whereby the display of goods for sale would not be considered an offer but only an invitation to treat (*Fisher v Bell* (1961)).

12.1.8 Advertisements

1. S5 of the TDA 1968 confirms that a person who publishes an advertisement which contains a false trade description may be guilty of offences under s1(1)(a) and s1(1)(b) of the Act.

2. S5 applies to advertisements, catalogues and price lists (s39(1)).

3. In determining whether goods are of a class to which a trade description used in an advertisement relates, regard shall be had to:
   - the form and content of the advertisement;
   - the time, place, manner and frequency of its publication; and
   - all other matters making it likely or unlikely that a person would think that the description applies to the goods.

4. As well as the general defence in s24, advertisers may have a defence under s25 of the Act (see section 12.4).

12.2 MISDESCRIPTION OF SERVICES

1. S14 creates two offences in relation to services. These are:
   (a) making a statement which the maker knows to be false; and
   (b) recklessly making a statement which is false about any services.

2. The statement must be in the course of any trade or business and can be about any of the following:
   - the provision of any services, accommodation or facilities;
   - the nature of any services, accommodation or facilities;
   - the time or manner of the provision of any services, accommodation or facilities, eg that a 24-hour service is provided;
   - the examination, approval or evaluation of any services, accommodation or facilities; eg AA approved;
   - the location or amenities of any accommodation, eg seaview, balcony or swimming pool, but note that the section does not apply to residential property. False statements about residential property are covered by the Property Misdescriptions Act 1991.

3. 'In the course of any trade or business' includes profession or a claim to have a professional qualification (*R v Breeze* (1973)).

4. A statement can be oral or written or pictorial, eg an artist's impression (*R v Clarkson Holidays* (1972)).

5. Statements which are forecasts or promises about the future are not covered by s14 (*Beckett v Cohen* (1972)), though there may be a breach of contract in such cases.

6. The statement must be false to a material degree (s14(4) TDA 1968).

12.2.1 Knowledge of falsity

1. The *mens rea* of the offence under s14(1)(a) is that the defendant knows that the statement is false. There is no need to prove that it was intended to mislead consumers.

2. This includes not only knowledge of the falsity at the time the statement was made, but also includes knowledge of the falsity which obtained subsequent to the first publication, if the statement continues to be published (*Wings Ltd v Ellis* (1985)).

12.2.2 Recklessness

1. The *mens rea* of the offence under s14(1)(b) is that the defendant was reckless as to whether the statement was false.

2. 'Reckless' in this area means 'not having enough regard for the truth' (*MFI Warehouses Ltd v Nattrass* (1973)).

3. Recklessness does not imply dishonesty, nor is it necessary to prove that the defendant deliberately closed his eyes to the true facts (*MFI Warehouses Ltd v Nattrass* (1973)).

12.3 DISCLAIMERS

1. Liability for an offence under s1 TDA 1968 can be avoided by the use of an effective disclaimer.

2. A disclaimer is a statement which makes it clear that the trade description cannot be relied on. It amounts to saying 'I am not making any representation at all' (*Wandsworth LBC v Bentley* (1980)).

3. For a disclaimer to be effective it must be 'as bold, precise and compelling as the trade description itself' and it must be communicated at or before the time of making the trade description (*Norman v Bennett* (1974)).
4. Very clear words are required, so that the misleading effect of the trade description is displaced, eg in *R v Hammertons Cars Ltd* (1976) where there was a false milometer reading on a car, it was said that the defendant must take positive steps to ensure that the customer understands that the reading is meaningless.
5. However, a disclaimer as to the mileage of a car was held not to be a defence where the defendant had personally turned back the odometer (*R v Southwood* (1987)).
6. A small inconspicuous notice is unlikely to be an effective disclaimer.
7. It is uncertain whether a disclaimer can be used in relation to an offence under s14 TDA 1968.

12.4 DEFENCES

1. S24(1) provides a general defence provided that the defendant can prove both:
   (a) that the commission of the offence was due to a mistake or to reliance on information supplied by another person or the act or default of another person, an accident or some other cause beyond his control; and
   (b) that he took all reasonable precautions and exercised all due diligence to avoid the commission of the offence by himself or any person under his control.
2. In this section the words 'another person' can include an employee (*Beckett v Kingston Bros (Butchers) Ltd* (1970)).
3. Where an employee commits the offence the company will be liable only if the employee is 'acting as the mind and will of the company' (*Tesco Supermarkets Ltd v Nattrass* (1971)).
4. This weakens the Act as it allows companies to escape prosecution since only senior managers and directors are

considered to be the 'mind and will of the company' (*Tesco Supermarkets Ltd v Nattrass* (1971)).

12.4.1 'All due diligence'

1. Reliance on a manufacturer's statement where it is easy to test the product is not considered as taking all reasonable precautions and exercising all due diligence (*Sharratt v Geralds* (1970)).
2. Reliance on the word of a previous owner of a car that the mileage was accurate was not regarded as taking all reasonable precautions and exercising all due diligence (*Simmons v Potter* (1975)).
3. The standard is probably higher for large retailers than for the village shop (*Garrett v Boots Chemists Ltd* (1980)).

12.4.2 Special defence to s1(1)(b)

1. S24(3) provides that 'it shall be a defence for the person charged to prove that he did not know, and could not with reasonable diligence have ascertained, that the goods did not conform to the description or that the description had been applied to the goods'.
2. This is a defence of innocent supply of goods.
3. It protects suppliers from prosecution where they had no way of discovering that either the description was false or that it had been applied to goods.

12.4.3 Innocent publication of an advertisement

S25 provides a defence for advertisers where they received the advertisement for publication in the ordinary course of business and did not know and had no reason to suspect that its publication would amount to an offence under the TDA 1968.

CHAPTER 13
MISLEADING PRICES

Consumer Protection Act 1987, Part III

S20(1) makes it an offence:
- for a person in the course of his business;
- to give to any consumers;
- an indication which is misleading as to the price;

at which any goods, services, accommodation or facilities are available.

S20(2): it is an offence if an indication as to price is given which later becomes misleading.

Codes of Practice

These exist for:
- price comparisons;
- actual price to the consumer;
- price indications which become misleading after they have been given;
- sale of new houses.

Regulations

These exist for:
- payment by credit card;
- bureaux de change;
- resale of tickets.

MISLEADING PRICES

Defences

CPA s39(1)
- if can show took all reasonable steps and exercised all due diligence to avoid committing the offence.

CPA s24:
- act authorised by Regulations;
- price indication made in media;
- innocent publisher;
- in relation to an indication of a recommended price, that it was misleading because of third party's failure to follow recommendation.

13.1 BACKGROUND

1. The Moloney Committee (1962) recommended that the problem of misleading prices should be tackled by including the price in the definition of trade description.
2. Instead of doing this, however, s11 of the Trade Descriptions Act 1968 created three offences:
   - false comparisons with a recommended price;
   - false comparisons with the trader's own previous price;
   - an indication that the price was less than that actually being charged.
3. This did not prevent malpractice, eg by traders setting unrealistically high recommended prices which they could then use to compare the sale price favourably.
4. The TDA offences only applied to goods: they did not apply to services, accommodation or facilities.
5. The Price Marking (Bargain Offers) Order 1979 attempted to clarify what indications were offences; it also applied to services but it was criticised for being so badly drafted that its provisions were not understandable.
6. Eventually both s11 of the Trade Descriptions Act 1968 and the Price Marking (Bargain Offers) Order 1979 were replaced by Part III of the Consumer Protection Act 1987.

13.2 THE CONSUMER PROTECTION ACT 1987, PART III

1. S20 of the CPA creates two offences. The first (s20(1)) is in respect of offences committed at the time of the misleading indications of price: the second (s20(2)) is in respect of indications which are accurate when first made but later become misleading.
2. S20(1) makes it an offence:
   - for a person in the course of his business;
   - to give to any consumers;
   - an indication which is misleading as to the price;

- at which any goods, services, accommodation or facilities are available.

3. S20(2) creates an offence where an indication as to price is given which later becomes misleading and no reasonable steps are taken to prevent consumers from relying on the indication.

4. S20 does not require goods to have been sold (or services etc supplied) to a consumer. The only requirement for an offence to have been committed is to show that the price indication is misleading.

13.2.1 'In the course of his business'

1. It has been held that a private members' club is not a business for the purposes of s20 (*John v Matthews* (1970)).

2. The use of 'his' business in s20 means that employees are not liable to be prosecuted under this section (*R v Warwickshire CC, ex parte Johnson* (1993)).

3. Proceedings can be brought personally against 'any director, manager, secretary, or other similar officer' of a body corporate where the company is guilty of an offence which was committed with consent or connivance of the officer or was attributable to their neglect (s40(2)).

4. Where there is a franchise, both franchiser and franchisee may be guilty (*Surrey CC v Burton Retail Ltd* (1998)).

13.2.2 'To any consumer'

1. 'Consumer' is defined by s20(6) as:
   (a) in relation to any goods, any person who might wish to be supplied with the goods for his own private use or consumption;
   (b) in relation to any services or facilities, any person who might wish to be provided with them otherwise than for the purposes of any business of his;
   (c) in relation to any accommodation, any person who might

wish to occupy the accommodation otherwise than for the purposes of any business of his.

2. S20 does not apply where a retailer buys from wholesaler (*Toys 'R' Us v Gloucestershire CC* (1994)).

3. Nor does s20 apply where the goods, by their nature, cannot have been intended for consumer use, eg dental equipment.

4. The fact that the misleading price indication is noticed by a Trading Standards Officer, rather than a consumer, does not prevent it from being an offence. It is not necessary to show that a consumer was actually misled.

13.2.3 An indication as to price

1. Indication is wider than the word 'representation'.

2. It has been held to be intended to 'extend over conduct or signs of many different kinds' (*Doble v David Greig Ltd* (1972)).

13.2.4 Price

1. Price is defined as 'the aggregate of the sums required to be paid by a consumer' (s20(6)).

2. This definition does not cover a rough estimate as this is not a sum 'required to be paid'.

3. However, a firm quotation is covered by s20 (*Gilbert and Partners v Knight* (1968)).

4. Price includes all aspects of the charge, eg *R v Kettering Magistrates Court, ex parte MRB Insurance Brokers* (2000) where the rate of interest was wrongly stated.

5. 'Aggregate' means that the price must make clear what is covered and failing to indicate an extra charge is an offence, eg for VAT (*Richards v Westminster Motors* (1976)) or for delivery (*Toyota (GB) v N Yorkshire CC* (1998)).

6. Price matching is covered, ie where a store promises to mach any lower price in another store (*DSG Retail Ltd v Oxfordshire CC* (2001)).

7. Price matching will be charged under s20(2) as the price only becomes misleading if the store refuses to honour its promise (*Link Stores Ltd v Harrow LBC* (2001)).

13.2.5 Misleading

1. Under s21(1) an indication is misleading if what is conveyed by the indication, or what consumers might reasonably be expected to infer from the indication, includes any of the following:
   (a) that the price is less than it in fact is, eg a price is shown on a shelf in a supermarket but a higher price charged at the till;
   (b) that the applicability of the price does not depend on facts or circumstances on which its applicability does in fact depend, eg a discount is available to all customers when it is only available to cash customers;
   (c) that the price covers matters in respect of which an additional charge is in fact made, eg appearing to include delivery when it does not;
   (d) that a person who in fact has no such expectation:
       (i) expects the price to be increased or reduced; or
       (ii) expects the price (or the price as increased or reduced) to be maintained, eg an introductory offer indicating that the price will increase later but the seller does not expect the price to increase;
   (e) a comparison with another price or value where the facts on which the comparison is based are misleading, eg 'reduced from £50' when the highest previous price was £45.
2. The opening words of s21 contain both subjective and objective tests as to whether the indication was misleading:
   • there is a **subjective** test as it applies if the effect of the indication actually misleads a consumer (*Doble v David Greig Ltd* (1972));
   • there is an **objective** test as the section also includes 'what

consumers might reasonably be expected to infer from the indication'.

3. 'Misleading' is limited to the matters in the list in s21(1). This limits the scope of s20. It would have been better to make the list merely illustrative to allow the courts to apply the all-embracing words of s20.

13.2.6 Goods, services, accommodation and facilities

1. S21(1) states that services or facilities are references to 'any services or facilities whatever'. It gives examples which include:
   - credit, banking or insurance services;
   - the purchase of foreign currency;
   - the supply of electricity;
   - the provision of off-street car parks;
   - arrangements for keeping caravans on land, unless occupied as the persons' main residence.
2. 'Accommodation' includes a new house or flat being sold by a builder or developer (s23). 'New' includes both new constructions and conversions of old buildings (unless the building has been used as a residence previously).
3. S20 also applies to accommodation in package holidays, but there are also separate regulations in respect of package holidays (see Chapter 15).

13.3 CODE OF PRACTICE

1. S25 gives the Secretary of State the power to approve a Code of Practice.
2. A code, *Code of Practice for Traders on Price Indications*, was issued in 1988.
3. The Code has four parts:
   - Part 1 Price comparisons;
   - Part 2 Actual price to the consumer;

- Part 3 Prices indications which become misleading after they have been given;
- Part 4 Sale of new houses.

4. If a trader contravenes the Code, the prosecution can rely on that fact to establish that an offence has been committed, but the contravention is not automatically an offence.

5. Compliance with the Code is evidence which can be used in defence, but does not automatically give a defence.

13.3.1 Comparisons

1. The Code of Practice gives general guidance on the use of comparisons.

2. It advises traders to avoid the use of language which suggests that a comparison is being made.

3. Where a comparison is made, the Code advises that it should be clear and abbreviations such as 'MRP' (manufacturer's recommended price) or 'ASP' (after sale price) should not be used. The exception is the abbreviation 'RRP' (recommended retail price) which is permitted.

4. Where a comparison is made with a previous selling price:
   - the previous price should be the last price charged;
   - the goods, service, accommodation or facility to which it refers should have been available at that outlet for at least 28 consecutive days in the six months immediately preceding the publication of the indication containing the comparison (the burden of proving this is on the trader);
   - the 28-day rule does not apply to food or other short shelf-life goods: for these, the comparison is the last price charged.

5. A trader may make a comparison with a manufacturer's recommended price, but only if:
   - it is the price recommended by the manufacturer as the sale price to consumers;
   - the trader deals with the manufacturer on commercial terms; and

- the price is not significantly higher than the price at which the product is sold generally.
6. Comparing with other traders' prices (eg '£10 cheaper than in X store') is permitted if the person giving the indication knows that the price quoted is accurate and up to date.

13.4 REGULATIONS

1. S26 of the CPA gives the Secretary of State power to issue regulations on misleading prices in specific areas.
2. Three sets of regulations have been issued. These are:
   - the Payment by Credit Card Price Indications (Method of Payment) Regulations 1991, under which customers must be made aware of any difference in price depending on the method of payment;
   - the Price Indications (Bureaux de Change) Regulations 1992 which require the selling and buying rate and any commission charges for currency to be displayed and also any differences between rates for travellers' cheques and notes. The information must be given 'clearly and prominently' and must be visible to consumers as they either approach or enter the bureau de change;
   - the Price Indications (Resale of Tickets) Regulations 1994 state that customers must be informed of the face value of tickets and any additional commission payable to the agency.

13.5 DEFENCES

1. There is a general 'due diligence' defence available for offences under both Part II and Part III of the CPA.
2. This makes it a defence for a person to show that he 'took all reasonable steps and exercised all due diligence to avoid committing the offence' (CPA, s39(1)). In *Berkshire CC v Olympic Holidays Ltd* (1994) this defence was successful where an unexplained fault on a computer caused a print-out of the wrong price. The software had been tested previously and the

same transaction later produced the correct price on a repeated test.

3. S24 provides four specific defences to offences against s20(1) and (2). These are where the defendant can prove:

- the acts or omissions were authorised by Regulations made under s26;
- the price indication was made in the media (other than in an advertisement);
- he was an innocent publisher or advertising agency who was unaware, and had no grounds for suspecting, that the advertisement contained a false price indication;
- the misleading price related to a recommended price of a supplier (not the price at which the item was available) and it was false only because of an unexpected failure of the supplier to follow the recommendation. (This defence is only available to a s20(1) offence.)

CHAPTER 14

CONSUMER CREDIT

Consumer Credit Act 1974

provides protection through:
- civil law;
- criminal sanctions;
- administrative control, especially licensing of credit providers.

Regulations provide detail in these areas.

Types of agreement

These include:
- hire-purchase;
- conditional sales;
- credit sales;
- consumer hire.

Regulated agreements are protected:
- also partially regulated agreements; and
- linked transactions.

CONSUMER CREDIT

Formalities

Pre-contractual disclosure:
- adequate information in adverts and quotations;
- provide copy of agreement (in some cases a second copy).

Contractual requirements
- in writing;
- document to be clear and legible;
- signed by debtor personally;
- all financial details must be shown together – these include:
  - APR;
  - amount of credit;
  - comparison of cash/credit cost;
  - total charge for credit;
  - total amount payable.

Rights of consumer

Withdrawal from agreement
- must be before creditor executes agreement.

Cancellation
- within 5 days of receipt of second copy of agreement;
- only when debtor has not signed at place of business.

Termination
- at any time before last instalment due;
- but remain liable for all payments due before termination;
- also, if less than half of price paid, can be required to pay the extra.

14.1 CONSUMER CREDIT ACT 1974

1. The Consumer Credit Act 1974 (CCA) is a comprehensive Act which, together with Regulations made under it, contains almost all consumer credit law. One exception is mortgages of personal property which are covered by the Bills of Sale Acts 1878–82.

2. The CCA provides protection through such ways as:
   - civil law, with Regulations concerning consumer credit agreements;
   - the power of the courts to alter extortionate credit transactions;
   - criminal sanctions for breach of certain laws;
   - administrative control in such matters as licensing.

3. The protection given by the Act covers 'individuals'. This is wider than 'consumers' in other areas of consumer law, as s189 states that 'individual' includes a partnership or other unincorporated body of persons.

4. The rights given to a debtor or hirer under the CCA cannot be removed or reduced.

5. The definition section of the CCA, s189, contains 177 definitions.

6. To help explain the law, Schedule 2 contains 24 worked examples.

14.2 DIFFERENT TYPES OF CREDIT AGREEMENT

1. Many different types of agreement come under the term 'consumer credit agreement'. They include:
   - hire-purchase;
   - conditional sale;
   - credit sale;
   - personal loan;
   - overdraft;

- loan secured by a mortgage on land (usually the debtor's home);
- credit card;
- pledges;
- budget accounts in shops.

14.2.1 Definitions of main types of credit agreement

1. A hire-purchase agreement is defined (s189) as an agreement:
   - under which goods are bailed (ie possession transferred by one person (the bailor) to another (the bailee) for a specific purpose) in return for periodical payments by the bailee; and
   - the ownership of the goods will pass to the bailee if the terms of the agreement are complied with; and one or more of the following occur:
     (i) the exercise of an option to purchase by the bailee; or
     (ii) the doing of any other specified act by any party to the agreement; or
     (iii) the happening of any other specified event.
2. A conditional sale agreement is defined (s189) as an agreement:
   - for the sale of goods or land;
   - under which the purchase price or part of it is payable by instalments; and
   - the ownership of the goods or land is to remain in the seller until such conditions as to the payment of instalments or as may be specified in the agreement are fulfilled.
3. A credit sale agreement is one where there is a sale of goods on credit terms but the ownership of the goods passes to the buyer immediately.
4. A consumer hire agreement is covered by the CCA if it is 'capable of subsisting for more than three months' (s15 CCA and *Dimond v Lovell* (2000)).

14.2.2 Other definitions

1. Consumer credit involves specialist terminology. Some of the main terms are explained below.
2. A restricted-use agreement (s11) is generally one in which the debtor can use the credit only for a certain purpose: it will perform one of the following three functions:
   - finance an agreement between the debtor and the creditor;
   - finance an agreement between the debtor and a supplier other than the creditor;
   - refinance an existing debt, eg a consolidation loan.
3. An unrestricted-use agreement is one where the debtor can use the amount loaned in any way.
4. Running-account credit is where the debtor may make withdrawals (up to an agreed amount) on the understanding that the debtor will top up his account. This includes the main credit card agreements under which the consumer can choose how much of his debt to repay at the end of each month. A running account qualifies as a consumer credit agreement if:
   - the debtor cannot draw more than the specified amount (£25,000) at any one time; or
   - a term unfavourable to the debtor (eg increasing the rate of interest) will become operative if the debit balance goes above a certain amount; or
   - at the time of the agreement it is unlikely that the debit balance will rise above the specified amount (£25,000).
5. Fixed sum credit is any personal credit agreement which is not a running-account credit agreement (s10(1)(b)). It includes loans for a specific purpose such as the acquisition of goods.
6. The total charge for credit includes:
   - the total of interest payments;
   - other charges payable at any time under the agreement. This includes the general costs of setting up the agreement as well as such matters as survey fees, legal fees or stamp duty);

- a £250 document fee (*Wilson v First County Ltd (No 2)* (2001)).

7. The total charge for credit is important because any sum which forms part of the total charge for credit is not included in the amount of credit and must, therefore, be ignored in deciding whether or not the credit exceeds the specified sum (£25,000).

8. The object of making the total charge for credit clear is so that potential borrowers can compare the cost of credit and 'shop around' for the best deal.

14.2.3 Debtor–creditor–supplier

There are three main ways in which goods can be acquired on credit. These are:

- where the goods and credit are obtained from the creditor;
- where the goods are acquired from a supplier who is connected to the creditor; (these first two are debtor–creditor–supplier (D–C–S) agreements);
- where there is no link between the creditor and the supplier, eg the debtor is lent money to use for whatever he wants. This is a debtor–creditor agreement.

14.3 THE SCOPE OF THE CCA

1. The CCA determines which consumer credit agreements are regulated.

2. As well as regulated agreements the Act also defines:
- partially regulated agreements;
- exempt agreements;
- linked transactions.

14.3.1 Regulated agreements

1. Regulated agreements are agreements which come within the definition of 'consumer credit agreement' (s8) or 'consumer hire agreement' (s15).

2. S8(2) defines a consumer credit agreement as an agreement whereby one person (the creditor) provides an individual (the debtor) with credit not exceeding £25,000.

3. S15 states that a consumer hire agreement has the following elements:
- a bailment of goods;
- by one person (the owner);
- to an individual (the hirer);
- where it is not hire-purchase;
- it is capable of lasting more than three months; and
- it does not require the hirer to make payments in excess of £25,000. (It is proposed in the Consumer Credit Bill 2004 that this limit will be abolished.)

4. If an agreement is within one of these definitions then it is regulated unless it is an exempt agreement.

14.3.2 Partially regulated agreements

1. There are two types of agreement which may be partially regulated. These are non-commercial agreements and small agreements.

2. A non-commercial agreement is one not made by the creditor or owner in the course of a business. Such agreements are not regulated in regard to formalities and cancellation.

3. A small agreement is one where the credit or the hire payments do not exceed £50.

14.3.3 Exempt agreements

1. Exempt agreements are set out in s16 and in the Consumer Credit (Exempt Agreements) Order 1989 (as amended).

2. The main category of exemption is agreements which relate to financing the purchase of land or the provision of a dwelling where the agreement is secured by a mortgage. The creditor must be a local authority or body named in the Regulations (eg insurance companies, friendly societies and charities).

3. Fixed-sum credit agreements are exempt if the number of payments is four or less, to be paid within 12 months of the date of the agreement.
4. Running-account credit agreements are exempt if the whole of the credit for a period is repayable by a single payment.
5. Debtor–creditor agreements are those offered to a class of person (eg employees), not to the public generally and, where the total charge for credit consists only of interest at not more than 1 per cent above base rate, are exempt agreements.

14.3.4 Linked transactions

1. Transactions which are linked to actual or prospective regulated agreements include:
   - the sale of a car in a D–C–S agreement where the creditor supplies the credit but the car is sold by the supplier;
   - a maintenance contract which the debtor/hirer has to enter into alongside the main agreement;
   - any agreement which induces the debtor/hirer to enter into the consumer credit agreement.
2. Rights are given to the debtor in a linked transaction for such matters as withdrawal, cancellation, early settlement and extortionate credit bargains.

14.4 FORMALITIES OF THE AGREEMENT

The CCA (and Regulations made under the Act) set down strict rules for formalities in consumer credit agreements. These cover:
- the pre-contractual period;
- the formation of the contract;
- rights to withdraw from the contract;
- rights of cancellation;
- rights on termination.

14.4.1 Pre-contractual disclosure

1. A creditor has to give adequate information in advertisements (s44).
2. A creditor has to give adequate information in quotations (s52).
3. Both these requirements are to allow the debtor or hirer to be aware of the commitment (s)he might be taking on.

14.4.2 Special pre-contractual requirements for land mortgages

1. Where an agreement to finance a land mortgage is a regulated agreement (ie it is for less than £25,000 and is not an exempt agreement) there are special pre-contractual requirements.
2. A pre-contractual consideration period has been created since a contract for land does not have the protection of cancellation rights in other consumer credit agreements.
3. This period has been created to allow consumers time to reflect, without pressure from the creditor, on whether they can really afford the commitment of the debt.
4. At least seven days before sending the agreement for signature, the creditor must give a copy of the agreement to the potential debtor.
5. This copy must contain a notice, in the prescribed form, clearly setting out the right to withdraw from the transaction and warning the potential debtor not to sign the actual agreement if they decide not to go ahead with it.
6. During the seven-day period the creditor must not contact the potential debtor.

14.4.3 Contractual requirements

1. There are three broad requirements (s61):
   - a document in the prescribed form containing all the prescribed terms and conforming to Regulations made

under s60(1) must be signed in the prescribed manner by both the debtor or hirer (personally) and by or on behalf of the creditor or owner; and

- the document must embody all the terms of the agreement other than implied terms (eg those implied by the Sale of Goods Act 1979); and
- the document must be, when presented or sent to the debtor or hirer for signature, in such a state that all its terms are readily legible.

2. The details required in consumer credit agreements are set out in the Consumer Credit (Agreements) Regulations 1983. These vary with the type of agreement.

3. The main requirements are that the document must contain (shown together as a whole and not interspersed among other information) details of the financial arrangements, including:

- the annual percentage rate of charge (APR);
- the amount of credit provided;
- a comparison of the cash price and the credit price;
- the total charge for credit;
- details of the amount and intervals of repayments;
- the total amount payable.

4. The document must be legible and the print in a colour which is easily distinguishable from the colour of the paper.

5. If an agreement is not properly executed then the creditor (or owner) cannot enforce it against the debtor (or hirer) unless:

- the court makes an order for enforcement; or
- the debtor (or hirer) consents to enforcement.

14.4.4 Copies of the agreement

1. The debtor or the hirer is always entitled to one copy of the agreement and in many cases the debtor or the hirer is entitled to two copies.

2. The right to a second copy depends on whether the agreement is presented or sent to him or dealt with in another way and whether the first copy has already been signed by the creditor or owner.

3. An agreement already signed by the creditor or owner when presented or sent to the creditor or hirer is an 'executed agreement'. One not already signed is an 'unexecuted agreement'.

4. Where the debtor or hirer is sent or presented with an unexecuted document then a second copy of the agreement must be sent or delivered to him within seven days of receiving the unexecuted agreement.

5. Where the document is an executed agreement there is no requirement for a second copy.

14.5 WITHDRAWAL

1. The normal contract rules on withdrawal of an offer apply. This means that a debtor (or hirer) can withdraw his/her offer at any time before it is accepted.

2. In addition, there is extra protection for regulated agreements, as the debtor is allowed to withdraw from a prospective agreement (s57).

3. S57 allows notice of the withdrawal to be given to a wide range of people. This includes the creditor (or hirer), the supplier or 'any person who, in the course of a business carried on by him, acts on behalf of the debtor or hirer in any negotiations for the agreement'.

4. The notice of withdrawal also extends to any linked transactions.

5. Where the debtor (or hirer) withdraws from an agreement, the parties are returned to the prior position, ie all goods and money must be returned.

14.6 CANCELLATION

1. A regulated agreement may be cancelled, provided that:
   - oral representations were made to the debtor (hirer) in his presence (any made by telephone cannot be relied on); and
   - the unexecuted agreement was not signed by the debtor (hirer) at business premises of the creditor or owner or any

party in a linked transaction.

2. The cancellation must be made within five days of receipt of the statutory second copy of the agreement.

3. Regulations require that a cancellation form must be included with the second copy of the agreement.

4. Notice of cancellation must be in writing (though no special form of words is required). The notice must be served on one of the following:
   - the creditor or owner;
   - the person specified in the copy of the agreement or in a cancellation form sent with the copy;
   - the agent of the creditor or owner.

5. A notice of cancellation which is posted takes effect from the date of posting.

6. When an agreement is cancelled, the effect is as though it (and any linked transactions) had never been made. The debtor (hirer) can therefore recover any payments already made and is discharged from further payments. Goods must be returned to the creditor (owner).

14.7 TERMINATION

1. The right to terminate is available only for regulated hire-purchase and conditional sales (ss99 and 100) and for consumer hire agreements.

2. Termination can be made at any time before the last instalment or payment is due.

14.7.1 Termination of hire-purchase and conditional sales

1. The termination only operates for the future, so that any money already due remains payable.

2. In addition, on early termination, the debtor may have to pay a further sum to bring the total payments up to one-half of the total price.

3. However, if the court is satisfied that a sum of less than one-half of the total price is adequate to cover the creditor's loss, the court may order a smaller sum to be paid. (This does not affect the sums due under the agreement to the date of termination. These remain due.)
4. On termination the debtor must allow the creditor to retake the goods.
5. There are two exceptions where termination is not available:
   - in a conditional sale agreement for land where the title of the land has passed to the debtor;
   - in a conditional sale of goods where the ownership of the goods has been transferred to a third party.

14.7.2 Termination of hire agreements

1. The earliest these can be terminated is 18 months after the making of the agreement (unless the contract provides for earlier termination).
2. The hirer must give a termination notice equal to the shortest payment interval or three months (whichever is less).
3. The right to terminate is not available where:
   - the total payments for the hire exceed £900 in any one year;
   - goods are let out for the hirer's business and were selected by the hirer and acquired by the owner, at the hirer's request, from a third party;
   - the hirer requires the goods to re-let them in the course of a business.

14.8 EARLY REPAYMENT

1. Under s94 a debtor has the right to complete the agreement ahead of time.
2. This can be done by serving a notice on the creditor and by paying all sums due, less any statutory rebate of the total charge.

3. Any such rebate is calculated based on the actual time for which the debtor received credit.

4. The Consumer Credit (Rebate on Early Settlement) Regulations 1983 contain the formulae for making such calculations.

14.9 TIME ORDER

1. Where the debtor or hirer has been served with a notice of default or where the creditor or owner brings proceedings to enforce a regulated agreement, the debtor or hirer can apply for a time order.

2. A time order has the effect of allowing the debtor more time to comply with his obligations under his contract with the creditor.

3. The power to grant a time order only relates to 'any sum owed', but where a creditor brings a possession action the balance of the loan can be treated as 'owed' (*Southern and District Finance v Barnes* (1995)).

4. Guidelines on the making of time orders were given in *Southern and District Finance v Barnes* (1995). Key points to be considered are:
   - whether it is just to make an order, considering all the circumstances and the position of the creditor as well as that of the debtor;
   - any order made should be for a specific time on account of temporary financial difficulty;
   - if an order is made, then the court should suspend any possession order while the time order is complied with.

14.10 PROTECTION FROM REPOSSESSION OF GOODS

1. Where there is a regulated hire-purchase or conditional sale agreement, s92 of the CCA prevents the creditor or the owner from entering any premises to repossess goods without an order of the court.

2. In hire-purchase or conditional sale agreements, goods become 'protected goods' where:
   - the debtor is in breach; and
   - he has not terminated the agreement; and
   - he has paid to the creditor at least one-third of the total price; and
   - the creditor retains ownership of the goods.
3. A creditor cannot recover possession of protected goods without a court order.

14.11 EXTORTIONATE CREDIT BARGAINS

1. A bargain may be considered an extortionate one where the payments are grossly exorbitant or the agreement otherwise contravenes ordinary principles of fair dealing (s138).
2. Factors which are considered when deciding if a bargain is extortionate include:
   - the prevailing interests at the time when the bargain was made;
   - factors affecting the debtor, such as age, health, business capacity and the extent to which he was under financial pressure;
   - factors affecting the creditor, such as his relationship with the debtor and the degree of risk undertaken by him;
   - the extent to which a linked transaction was reasonably required for the protection of the debtor or the creditor.
3. Where a court decides that the bargain is extortionate, it has wide powers. It may:
   - direct accounts to be taken;
   - set aside obligations imposed on the debtor;
   - order sums to be repaid to the debtor;
   - order property given as security to be returned;
   - re-write the terms of the agreement.

14.12 PROPOSALS FOR REFORM

1. The Consumer Credit Bill 2004 proposes changes to the law to give consumers more protection.

2. The Bill will abolish the £25,000 limit so that consumer credit agreements of any value are covered.

3. The Bill will also introduce an improved system of licensing for credit agencies.

4. The proposed main changes to protect consumers are:

- the creditor will have to provide the debtor with an annual statement of the amount owed;
- the creditor will have to issue a notice of arrears where either four weekly payments have not been made or two payments where the interval of payment is more than a week;
- the concept of extortionate credit bargain will be abolished and replaced with the concept of unfair relationship;
- the unfairness can be in relation to the terms of the agreement, the way in which the creditor exercises or enforces his rights or any other thing done by the creditor before or after the making of the agreement;
- the court will have wide powers in respect of any agreement where there is found to be an unfair relationship.

CHAPTER 15

PACKAGE HOLIDAYS

Definition:
- broad definition in reg 2(1);
- prearranged combination of two of – transport, accommodation, other tourist services;
- must be sold at inclusive price, be for more than 24 hours and include accommodation.

Necessary information:
- by reg 9(1) must be given before contract concluded – contained in Schedule 2:
  - intended destination;
  - means of travel;
  - exact dates/places of departure;
  - locality/classification of accommodation;
  - meals included;
  - minimum number of travellers;
  - relevant itineraries;
  - name and address of organiser, retailer and insurer;
  - price and details for revising it;
  - payment schedule/method;
  - other necessary details;
  - method and period for complaints.

PACKAGE HOLIDAYS

Liability:
- by reg 15(1) is strict;
- unless not the fault of organiser (*Hartley v Inatasun*);
- ABTA Code requires liability for all agents and subcontractors;
- right to alterations is contractual – but if non-performance then is breach – BTA Code requires offer of suitable alternatives;
- passengers denied travel because of overbooking are entitled to a choice of:
  - reimbursement of the cost of the ticket;
  - re-routing to the destination at the earliest convenience;
  - re-routing at a later date at the passenger's convenience;
- reg 16(1) – organiser must have sufficient funds to pay back if insolvent;
- damages represent difference between contract quality and holiday quality: *Jackson v Horizon Holidays*;
- but possible to claim for mental distress: *Jarvis v Swan Tours*.

15.1 INTRODUCTION

1. There are various common-law protections in the case of holidays (see the 'holiday cases' in section 2.5.6).

2. However, the main area of consumer protection in the case of package holidays are the Package Travel, Package Holidays and Package Tours Regulations 1992 and also the ABTA Code of Practice.

3. The Regulations were introduced to comply with EU Directive 90/314 on Package Holidays and Package Tours.

4. The Directive was inevitable because of the level of tourism across EU member states.

5. Most consumer problems related to holidays concern differences between the holiday description on booking and the reality.

6. It is possible in these circumstances that there is also an offence under s14 Trade Descriptions Act 1978.

15.2 THE PACKAGE TRAVEL, PACKAGE HOLIDAYS AND PACKAGE TOURS REGULATIONS 1992

15.2.1 The definition of 'package holidays'

1. The Regulations do not alter the existing common-law protections but add significant duties on tour operators

2. The Regulations apply to all package holidays – but the word 'package' is given a very broad definition in regulation 2(1): 'the prearranged combination of at least two of the following components when sold or offered for sale at an inclusive price and when the service covers a period of more than 24 hours or includes overnight accommodation:
(a) transport
(b) accommodation

(c) other tourist services not ancillary to transport or
   accommodation and accounting for a significant
   proportion of the package and
   i. submission of separate accounts for different
      components shall not cause the arrangement to be other
      than a package;
   ii. the fact that a combination is arranged at the request of
      the consumer in accordance with his specific
      instructions (whether modified or not) shall not of itself
      cause it to be treated as other than pre-arranged.'

15.2.2 Information to be given by the holiday operator before the contract is concluded

1. Again, the basic common-law rules on formation can apply.
2. The brochure is generally seen as an invitation to treat.
3. But the Regulations, in regulation 9, provide certain
   safeguards by ensuring that certain information is given to the
   consumer before the contract is concluded, and that the
   information is comprehensible to the consumer.
4. The necessary information is detailed in Schedule 2:
   - the intended destination;
   - the intended means of travel;
   - the exact dates and the places of departure;
   - the locality of accommodation and its classification;
   - meals that are included in the package;
   - the minimum number of travellers to allow the holiday
     to go ahead;
   - any relevant itineraries, visits or excursions;
   - the names and full addresses of the organiser, retailer and
     insurer;
   - the price and any details with regard to revising the price;
   - the payment schedule and method of payment;
   - any other necessary details, such as specific arrangements
     for diet etc, that have been indicated by the consumer;
   - the method and period for complaints to be made.

5. This information must be given to the consumer both before the contract is made (reg 9(1)(b)) and in the contract itself (reg 9(1)(a)) (but this will not apply to very late bookings).
6. Failure to comply is a breach under regulation 9(3) and the operator is then prevented from relying on terms that are not sufficiently explained in this way – and the consumer may also cancel the holiday.

15.3 STATEMENTS MADE IN HOLIDAY BROCHURES

1. The common-law distinctions between terms and 'trade puffs' applies where no reasonable person could rely on the statement (*Hoffman v Intasun* (unreported) (1990)).
2. But in any case, by regulation 4, holiday operators will be liable if they supply misleading information in their descriptive matter.

15.4 LIABILITY

15.4.1 Terms and performance of the contract

1. Terms may be implied according to the 'officious bystander' test.
2. By regulation 15(1) the operator is liable for the improper performance of the contract by other service providers – so this is a form of strict liability on the operator to provide the service that the consumer contracted for.
3. The only exception is where the improper performance is neither the fault of the operator nor of any other service provider:
   - including where it is the fault of the consumer *Hartley v Intasun* (1987);
   - or where it is caused by the unforeseeable and unavoidable act of a third party; and
   - where *force majeure* applies, eg hurricanes.

4. The ABTA Code of Practice also requires that it should be a term of all contracts for package holidays that the operator will accept liability for the acts or omissions of their employees, agents, sub-contractors and suppliers which results in death, injury or illness – and that the operators will offer advice, guidance and financial assistance of up to £5,000 to consumers on holiday who suffer death, injury or illness.

15.4.2 Alterations to the holiday

1. Alteration depends on the terms of the contract – a common term allows alteration to the itinerary.
2. If an alteration amounts to non-performance then it is a breach of the contract by the operator and will be classed as a breach of a condition allowing the consumer to repudiate and claim back the cost of the holiday.
3. The ABTA Code Clause 2.4 requires operators to offer suitable alternatives in the case of cancellation or alteration.

15.4.3 Overbooking of flights

1. Passengers who are denied travel because of overbooking are entitled to a choice of:
   - reimbursement of the cost of the ticket;
   - re-routing to the destination at the earliest moment;
   - re-routing at a later date, at the passenger's convenience.
2. Passengers are also entitled to compensation.
3. Passengers are also entitled to free telephone or fax, hotel accommodation and refreshments if necessary.

15.4.4 Insolvency of the tour operator

1. The Package Travel, Package Holidays and Package Tours Regulations 1992 apply.
2. Under regulation 16(1), tour operators must at all times be able to satisfy evidence of sufficient funds to be able to return deposits in the event of insolvency.

3. Consumers who pay by credit card are also protected under the Consumer Credit Act 1974.

4. ABTA bonding arrangements ensure that a consumer is not left stranded when a tour operator goes into insolvency during his/her holiday.

15.4.5 Remedies

1. Damages are generally awarded on the basis of difference in value between what was contracted for and what was provided (*Jackson v Horizon Holidays Ltd* (1975)).

2. Incidental losses, such as payment for meals where the food provided was unacceptable, are also possible (*Davey v Cosmos* (1989)).

3. It is accepted that in the event of breach, return of the cost of the holiday may be insufficient damages – so awards for mental distress are also possible (*Jarvis v Swan Tours Ltd* (1973)).

4. Claims are also possible for physical discomfort (*Cook v Spanish Holidays* (1960)).

5. In any case, the operator is responsible for all losses that naturally flow from the breach, in accordance with the principle in *Hadley v Baxendale* (1854).

15.5 RECENT DEVELOPMENTS

1. The Office of Fair Trading (OFT) issued guidance to operators in March 2004.

2. The OFT believes that many standard-form terms in holiday contracts fall short of the requirements of the Unfair Terms in Consumer Contracts Regulations 1999 and has suggested alternative wording for operators to avoid liability.

3. These include standard terms on:
   - responsibility for errors and changes in invoices or brochures;
   - acceptance of responsibility for statements made by agents, employees and representatives;

- right to transfer holiday when prevented from travelling;
- price revision clauses;
- rights on cancellation and alteration;
- the right to compensation and the amount of compensation;
- cancellation by the consumer;
- cancellation charges for failure to pay deposit or balance;
- rights where services not supplied during the holiday;
- exclusions of liability;
- reporting of complaints;
- 'read and understand' declarations.

INDEX